Cockatiels For Dummies®

When to Clip Your Cockatiel's Wing Feathers

Here's how you know that it's time to clip your cockatiel's wing feathers:

- When your friend is gliding about the room easily. That may mean there's only one grown-out feather on each wing to trim, but that's all it takes for a cockatiel to have a great deal of airlift.

- When your cockatiel is at the end of one of her twice-a-year molts. She will have grown in new wing feathers. If you haven't noticed, she may not have noticed, either. But eventually she'll discover that she has the power of flight back again.

- When your male cockatiel is being uppity with you. He can reach high heights and look down on you, but you can't reach him. He's snappy and controlling. Clipping his wings will make him rely on you again for transportation and will soften his tone.

- If you just got your cockatiel and the bird's feathers have never been trimmed. You'll develop the closest relationship with your bird if she is easy for you to control and if she needs you. With clipped wings, she does need you to get off the floor and up to safer heights. She also needs you to go from room to room. When she needs to go somewhere, you're the one who can get her there. She just has to figure out how to ask. That fosters trust and communication, especially when both of you are successfully getting your points across.

- If you need to trim back an occasional stray feather that grows in out of turn.

When to Clip Your Cockatiel's Nails

You should clip your bird's nails on an as-needed basis, but here's how you know for sure when it's time for a trim:

- If the youngest and oldest members of the family can't hold the family pet without getting scratched or bruised. Their skin is the most sensitive, and holding a cockatiel may be painful for these members of the family unless her nails are clipped.

- If the nails are getting snagged in your sweaters or in your carpeting. They're just too long for the cockatiel's own safety.

- If an errant nail is getting long and threatens to grow up into the pad of your cockatiel's foot. Your cockatiel never kicks back and puts her feet up, so her feet need to be in excellent shape. If a long toenail or two threatens her comfort, then it's time to take care of those nails.

- If you can see visually that they are too long. When she perches, they wrap around each other. When she walks on a flat surface, they force her feet up off the surface instead of just touching it.

- If your cockatiel has a foot injury or defect that prevents her from perching normally. Without wear and perching, her nails may grow too long.

Cockatiels For Dummies®

Cheat Sheet

Poisonous Plants

Here are plants that are poisonous to your cockatiel:

- Avocado
- Black locust
- Clematis
- Diffenbachia
- Eggplant
- Foxglove
- Hemlock
- Lily of the valley
- Lobelia
- Lupine
- Crown vetch
- Oleander
- Philodendron
- Poinsettia
- Rhododendron
- Rhubarb leaves
- Virginia creeper
- Yew

Safe Houseplants for Your Cockatiel

Your cockatiel can safely live with the following plants:

- African violet
- Aloe
- Baby's tears
- Bamboo
- Begonia
- Christmas cactus
- Ferns
- *Ficus benjamina*
- Figs
- Grape ivy
- Herbs
- Monkey plant
- Mother-in-law's tongue
- Palms
- Peperomia
- Pothos
- Purple passion vine
- Schefflera
- Spider plant
- Swedish ivy
- Wandering Jew
- Zebra plant

Harmful Substances

Many cosmetic and cleaning substances are harmful to your cockatiel. Here are some things that can be dangerous to birds:

- Aerosol sprays
- Smoke, including cigarette smoke
- Cleaners
- Gas emitted from nonstick cookware when it's overheated (over 530 degrees F)
- Hair spray
- Natural gas leak
- New carpet odor
- Pesticides
- Room fresheners
- Rug cleaner
- Scented candles
- Self-cleaning-oven spray

Copyright © 2001 Wiley Publishing, Inc.
All rights reserved.

Item 5311-9.

For more information about Wiley Publishing, call 1-800-762-2974.

For Dummies: Bestselling Book Series for Beginners

Praise For Cockatiels For Dummies

This is the book I wish *I'd* written. *Cockatiels For Dummies* is your passport to cockatiel college! Diane Grindol's extensive knowledge and experience with these captivating creatures is peppered with her obvious love and understanding of the species. This is *the* reference book for new or experienced cockatiel connoisseurs: great information, user-friendly format, and no-nonsense style. Don't bring your new cockatiel home without it!

— Susan Chamberlain
Columnist, *Bird Talk*
Contributor: BIRDS USA, Pet Product News
President, Long Island Parrot Society

Cockatiels

FOR

DUMMIES®

by Diane Grindol

WILEY

Wiley Publishing, Inc.

Cockatiels For Dummies®

Published by
Wiley Publishing, Inc.
111 River St.
Hoboken, NJ 07030
www.wiley.com

Copyright © 2001 by Wiley Publishing, Inc., Indianapolis, Indiana

Published simultaneously in Canada

For general information on our other products and services or to obtain technical support, please contact our Customer Care Department within the U.S. at 800-762-2974, outside the U.S. at 317-572-3993, or fax 317-572-4002.

Wiley also publishes its books in a variety of electronic formats. Some content that appears in print may not be available in electronic books.

Library of Congress Control Number: 00-112143

ISBN: 0-7645-5311-9

Manufactured in the United States of America

10 9 8

1B/RV/QU/QV/IN

About the Author

Diane Grindol has been a regular columnist for the leading companion bird magazine, *Bird Talk,* since 1995. She is also the author of *The Complete Book of Cockatiels.* Diane speaks at bird clubs and seminars, and puts on educational seminars for pet bird owners. To date her "FeatherEd" seminars have been produced in Monterey, San Jose, Seattle and Chicago.

Diane Grindol grew up in Rolling Meadows, a suburb of Chicago, Illinois. In that section of town, most of the streets were named after birds; she wonders if this had an influence on her later life! In high school, Diane was an AFS exchange student to Turkey one summer. She studied French and art at William Woods College in Fulton, Missouri, including a junior year abroad in Nantes, France. Diane made two subsequent trips to Europe to bike, travel, study, and work. After moving to Monterey, California, in 1982, she met a spunky little male cockatiel named Clement and soon after acquired a gray hen of her own. Life hasn't been the same since! Diane wrote a pet column for the American Cockatiel Society for six years, and during that time produced some videos on cockatiel care and (x-rated) breeding. In 1988, she started contributing photos and editorial content to *Bird Talk* and other magazines. She founded the Monterey Bay Cage Bird Club in 1988, and was its program coordinator until it folded in 1999. As a cockatiel enthusiast, Diane was intrigued by the cockatiel research at U.C. Davis in California. She visited the facility in the late 1980s, wrote about it, and in 1993, assisted field biologist Dr. Ann Brice with studies of Amazon parrots in the wild in Guatemala. Diane published *Bird World* magazine for two years in the 1990s.

Diane's activities in the world of birds have concentrated on educating companion bird owners and empowering them to join her in adding to our knowledge about companion birds by contributing to research and conservation efforts. She feels we live in a powerful time for companion birds, when important discoveries are being made in avian medical research, companion animal studies, and in the biology of wild parrots. We live among giants and legends, among people making outstanding contributions and building the future for both us and our companion birds. As companion bird owners, we are also making those contributions, sharing what we observe of life with companion parrots who are one or two generations removed from the rain forest. We can all contribute to spreading general knowledge of bird care and behavior.

Diane has a small flock of cockatiels at home, including her original hen Dacey and five generations of descendents. They are joined by blue-headed Pionus "Aztec" and an apricot canary named "Skippy." Guinea pigs, Blossom and Buttercup, love bird veggies as much as the rest of the flock. Diane works full time for Web site www.catalogcity.com. She is a freelance writer, photographer, and pet sitter and a Companion Bird Consultant.

About Howell Book House

Committed to the Human/Companion Animal Bond

Thank you for choosing a book brought to you by the pet experts at Howell Book House, a division of Wiley Publishing, Inc. And welcome to the family of pet owners who've put their trust in Howell books for nearly 40 years!

Pet ownership is about relationships — the bonds people form with their dogs, cats, horses, birds, fish, small mammals, reptiles, and other animals. Howell Book House/Wiley Publishing understands that these are some of the most important relationships in life, and that it's vital to nurture them through enjoyment and education. The happiest pet owners are those who know they're taking the best care of their pets — and with Howell books owners have this satisfaction. They're happy, educated owners, and as a result, they have happy pets, and that enriches the bond they share.

Howell Book House was established in 1961 by Mr. Elsworth S. Howell, an active and proactive dog fancier who showed English Setters and judged at the prestigious Westminster Kennel Club show in New York. Mr. Howell based his publishing program on strength of content, and his passion for books written by experienced and knowledgeable owners defined Howell Book House and has remained true over the years. Howell's reputation as the premier pet book publisher is supported by the distinction of having won more awards from the Dog Writers Association of America than any other publisher. Howell Book House/Wiley Publishing has over 400 titles in publication, including such classics as The American Kennel Club's *Complete Dog Book,* the *Dog Owner's Home Veterinary Handbook, Blessed Are the Brood Mares,* and *Mother Knows Best: The Natural Way to Train Your Dog.*

When you need answers to questions you have about any aspect of raising or training your companion animals, trust that Howell Book House/Wiley Publishing has the answers. We welcome your comments and suggestions, and we look forward to helping you maximize your relationships with your pets throughout the years.

Dominique C. De Vito
Publisher
Howell Book House/Wiley Publishing, Inc.

Dedication

To Dacey in her grace and acceptance, my gray cockatiel hen who started it all; and to the community of friends who support my writing and interests: Bev, Doris, Linda, Judy, Tani and Tawny. They've been understanding about the hours and weekends I was glued to the keyboard instead of socializing or playing; they've pitched in when my bird interests take me away from my flock so that I know the birds are well cared for; they've listened, offered support, and questioned just enough to keep learning fun.

Author's Acknowledgments

I appreciate the opportunity to add a book about cockatiels to the *For Dummies* series. It is in-line with my dedication to making bird care information widely available. There's a special place in my heart for cockatiels, the number one companion bird in the U.S. for very good reasons! I must thank from the bottom of my heart my editors at Wily Publishing and Howell Book House: Tim Gallan, Kira Sexton, Scott Prentzas Nikki Moustaki, and Beth Adelman, for bringing this book to fruition.

Thanks to David Marak for getting in touch with me just as we were looking for an illustrator. You'll enjoy his work in this book.

Thanks to Bonnie Kenk for the knowledge and insight she added to this book as a technical editor. Bonnie has been both an inspiration and a sounding board over the years. Bonnie consistently develops successful projects backed by her heart and beneficial to both birds and their owners.

As I've grown in my understanding of companion birds over the years, I have had the opportunity to learn from many exceptional, talented and dedicated people. I appreciate the work, counse,l and friendship of numerous "bird people," including Dr. Mike Murray, Tom Roudybush, Dr. Irene Pepperberg, Dr. Branson Ritchie, Dr. Ann Brice, Chris Davis, Sally Blanchard, Liz Wilson, Layne Dicker, Tani Robar, Laurella Desborough, Joanne Abramson, Chris Shank, Jo Miller-Cole, Jeanne Sangster, and Therese Baker. I love you all!

I must acknowledge the communities of people who support me in my personal growth and in my everyday life. A book isn't a life; it's a project that is made possible by the people around me. Thanks to my patient coworkers at Altura International, who are enthusiastic about my sometimes double life as an employee and author. Thanks to photo models Ron Lynch, Sara Oliva, Troy Wilson, Jen Hattori, Bev Owens, and Greg Brown. Thanks as well to coworkers Anne Marie, Steffie, Tawny, Peter, Kylie, and Beth, and to the understanding of Val and Lee. Thanks to Landmark Education Corporation, where the people and the work inspire and challenge me. I owe special thanks to Bob and Genevieve Muson for their encouragement and acknowledgment, and to their dedication to the Wisdom course. Thanks as well to the friendly and welcoming members of the First Presbyterian Church of Monterey, including Lori Hughes and Pastors Sarah and Dwight Nave and Jay Bartow. Thanks to my bird sitters Judy Murphy, Bev Owens, and Linda Massolo. They make it possible for me to attend seminars and to speak about my passion to groups of bird lovers, secure in the knowledge that my birds at home are cared for well.

Publisher's Acknowledgments

We're proud of this book; please send us your comments through our Online Registration Form located at www.dummies.com/register.

Some of the people who helped bring this book to market include the following:

Acquisitions, Editorial, and Media Development

Senior Project Editor: Tim Gallan

Acquisitions Editors: Scott Prentzas, Kira Sexton

Senior Copy Editor: Tina Sims

Technical Editor: Bonnie Kenk

Editorial Manager: Pam Mourouzis

Editorial Assistant: Carol Strickland

Illustrator: David Marak

Interior Photos: Diane Grindol (unless otherwise noted)

Cover Photos: Bonnie Jay

Composition

Project Coordinator: Nancee Reeves

Layout and Graphics: Amy Adrian, Brian Drumm, Brent Savage, Jacque Schneider, Jeremey Unger

Proofreaders: Laura Albert, Marianne Santy, TECHBOOKS Production Services

Indexer: TECHBOOKS Production Services

Publishing and Editorial for Consumer Dummies

Diane Graves Steele, Vice President and Publisher, Consumer Dummies

Joyce Pepple, Acquisitions Director, Consumer Dummies

Kristin A. Cocks, Product Development Director, Consumer Dummies

Michael Spring, Vice President and Publisher, Travel

Brice Gosnell, Associate Publisher, Travel

Suzanne Jannetta, Editorial Director, Travel

Publishing for Technology Dummies

Andy Cummings, Vice President and Publisher, Dummies Technology/General User

Composition Services

Gerry Fahey, Vice President of Production Services

Debbie Stailey, Director of Composition Services

Contents at a Glance

Cartoons at a Glance

By Rich Tennant

"The birds diet is regulated pretty carefully, except when Doug falls asleep after dinner with his mouth open."

page 37

"I really don't think there's anything funny about teaching the cockatiel to sing the theme song from 'Mission Impossible' everytime I use my Ab-Cruncher."

page 111

"He loves his ball and string, but once in a while he'll pick up the trombone and play 'Under Paris Skies' over and over again."

page 177

"Now there's an attractive man you should go talk to. He's got a healthy plumage, his eyes and nostrils appear clear of debris and discharge and I love the cinnamon, pearl and grey markings of his necktie."

page 5

"It's 'Feathers', I think she's taking steroids."

page 157

Cartoon Information:
Fax: 978-546-7747
E-Mail: richtennant@the5thwave.com
World Wide Web: www.the5thwave.com

Table of Contents

Introduction

*W*elcome to *Cockatiels For Dummies*. My first assumption in writing this book is that you're anything but a dummy. You're smart enough to know that there is a lot to learn about a commonly kept pet bird, the cockatiel. If you're reading this book before you acquire your companion cockatiel, I'm especially happy. If you already have your cockatiel, you're off to a very good start on having a long and happy relationship. Congratulations!

I'm happy to share what it is like to live with these charmers. They've added immeasurably to my life. I've lived with anywhere from 1 to 30 of them for the past 18 years. Several of my current birds, including 18½-year-old Dacey, have been with me for a decade or longer. We're good friends. We've made good human friends in the bird community, as well. We've been advisors to the American Cockatiel Society pet owners. We've been cockatiel breeders, raising little fluff balls through their gangly porcupine-stage to feathered fledglings. Then we've watched those babies go to new homes. We exhibited cockatiels and won major points and prizes. Dacey's pearl daughter Mathilda has been across the country a couple times earning championship status and placing 2nd in the cockatiel division at the National Cage Bird Show. We've been photographers and writers. (Do my birds blink when a flash goes off? Not any more!) My cockatiels rather like this writing phase of our life together. They play happily on their cage or on the computer monitor, with Mom at home to supervise their forays onto forbidden curtains and to dole out treats and scratches. So the writing process takes a little longer than if I worked alone. I can't help but stop to watch their antics and take part. But that's what it's all about!

Cockatiels and I have had a long relationship. The most important thing I've learned is that there is still so much to learn! That became apparent all over again as I was writing this book. I'm frustrated by what we don't know about avian medicine, bird behavior, and the natural history of a bird that is a common species both in the wild and in aviculture. We have a lot to discover, which makes living in this day and age very exciting. During your years of cockatiel ownership, important information will come to light and new developments will shape the relationship between you and your cockatiel. Watch for it and take the opportunity to make it happen.

Cockatiels and You

All it takes to love a cockatiel is to know one. I was smitten by an outgoing gray male almost two decades ago, and my life hasn't been the same since. Chances are good that one of these crested charmers grabbed hold of your

_____

heart strings and it was all over for you, too. Cockatiels are charming, but they also have personality and willfulness. They're messy. They're social creatures who need your attention on a regular basis. You need to examine your lifestyle with an open mind before deciding that a cockatiel is the pet for you.

Cockatiels are among the least expensive parrots you can buy. That doesn't make their upkeep inexpensive, however. A bill from an avian veterinarian is the same for a cockatiel as it is for a large parrot. Cages and supplies are costly, and you shouldn't skimp on a cockatiel's diet. The care and feeding you give your cockatiel will ensure that you have 20 years together. That's more years for the investment than you'll have with most dogs or cats.

But cockatiels aren't dogs or cats. You'll need to put aside much of what you know about pet care and training to work with your bird. Happy bird owners know that theirs is an intellectual relationship built on trust. Cockatiels daily test your patience as well as bringing hilarity and joy to your life. I've armed you in this book with much of the knowledge you'll need to develop a good relationship with your cockatiel.

How This Book Is Organized

Cockatiels For Dummies is divided into four parts. It covers the basics of bird ownership as well as the finer points you're likely to wonder about once you've had a cockatiel for a while. You can skip around if you're an "advanced" cockatiel owner. Or you can review the basics. It never hurts. Your cockatiel's needs, health, safety, and behavior are covered. Whether you're reading from front to back or picking out the parts of this book in which you have a special interest, the following sections cover what you'll find in each part of this book.

Part 1: So You Think You'll Get a Cockatiel

This is where you discover what it's really like to live with a cockatiel — the mess and the wolf whistles. Some misconception about birds are explained and debunked, such as "birds are easy to care for." You'll figure out soon enough why that isn't true! Some of the differences between common pets and cockatiels are discussed, as well as the differences between cockatiels and other birds. If you're making a decision about whether to buy a bird, or what kind of bird to buy, you'll have some ammunition in this section.

There are also guidelines for choosing a cockatiel. Not just any cockatiel, but the best cockatiel for you. You'll want to consider the source, consider offering a "used" cockatiel a home, and consider what you want your relationship with your cockatiel to be. I cover some of the details of cockatiel selection, such as the color mutations available, and I help you decide on a name and figure out the cost of your new pet.

Part II: Cockatiel Care

Once the first glow of ownership is over, there are mundane tasks involved in caring for your cockatiel. These tasks are enumerated for you. As a new or established cockatiel owner, they give you ideas that will make cockatiel ownership fun. When you're looking for a cage, you'll find guidelines on picking out a cage that is right for both you and your cockatiel. There is a list of other supplies you can buy for your cockatiel, many of which can make care easier for you. I also cover the fundamentals of a good cockatiel diet, and I show you how to take care of your bird's grooming and socialization.

Part III: Behavior and Training

It's helpful to understand what behaviors are normal in healthy cockatiels. This knowledge will save you some panic attacks as you observe your cockatiel over the first weeks and months. I also show you how to train your cockatiel to follow simple commands, and I provide advice on how to deal with behavior problems.

Part IV: Keeping Cockatiels Healthy

This part deals with keeping a companion cockatiel both healthy and happy. I describe the various toxins and dangers that lurk in your very home, with the aim of helping you to prevent accidents. Cockatiels are curious and accidents do happen. My hope is that you can benefit from an awareness of the kind of predicaments a cockatiel is likely to get into.

You are an important observer of your cockatiel's health. Clues to illness in a cockatiel are listed in this part, with some advice on first aid you can give your cockatiel until he gets professional veterinary care. Some common cockatiel illnesses are discussed, as well as explanations of the signs of major disease.

Part V: The Part of Tens

Every ...*For Dummies* book ends with top-ten lists. They're fun, after all. I offer you ten mistakes that can spoil cockatiel ownership and ten New Year's resolution for having the best relationship with your cockatiel.

Icons Used In This Book

In ...*For Dummies* books, we use little pictures, or icons, in the margins to help you figure out important points in the chapter. Here's a brief explanation of the icons in this book:

When you see this icon read the text carefully. It means that paying attention to this information could save you or your cockatiel from misfortune. There is something dangerous that you should be aware of in this chapter, and this is it.

This icon points out useful information that will make life easier for you and your cockatiel. You can take the advice or leave it, but read it!

Important information is posted under this icon. It deserves a few neurons in your memory bank or a bookmark.

This information is "extra" because you and your cockatiel will get along fine without knowing in-depth facts about a topic. If you're in a hurry, skip these facts. If you're into trivia or science, look for them.

Getting in Touch with Diane

The really weird part about being an author is putting your heart and soul into your writing and thus feeling vulnerable. It's as though a great number of people can see into your soul and know what you care about the most. When there's no feedback, you don't know if baring your soul has touched anyone else or not! I guess it's a little more rewarding in that way to be a performer with instant feedback. If you feel inclined to tell me about living with your particular cockatiel, I will read your account with delight. I have both an e-mail and snail mail address. I won't promise to answer every inquiry or letter, but will do my best! Watch for my monthly column in *Bird Talk* magazine or my presentations at a seminar near you. You can send an e-mail to me at tiels@redshift.com or write to this address:

Diane Grindol
P.O. Box 51247
Pacific Grove, CA 93950

Part I
So You Think You'll Get a Cockatiel

The 5th Wave By Rich Tennant

"Now there's an attractive man you should go talk to. He's got a healthy plumage, his eyes and nostrils appear clear of debris and discharge and I love the cinnamon, pearl and grey markings of his necktie."

In this part . . .

1 give you guidelines for choosing the best cockatiel. I show you what sources are available for finding bird companions, and I cover what it's like to live with and care for a cockatiel.

Chapter 1

Living with a Personable Pet Cockatiel

Cockatiels are small parrots native to the Australian desert with a charming, inquisitive disposition. They're calm and cuddly when hand-fed as babies or when raised with frequent handling and socialization. They're large enough to be handled easily but small enough so that their cage doesn't take up a lot of room and that exploring our homes provides a cockatiel with adequate exercise. Cockatiels come in many colors — all variations of gray, brown, white, and yellow — so there is one for almost every taste. Most of the color mutations sport handsome orange cheek patches, so they have permanent makeup, saving the fuss of applying rouge! Cockatiels are long and slim, with long wings, a slim body, and a long tail.

I can't think of a better way to start cockatiel ownership than reading about the feathered being you're bringing into your life. If this is your first bird, you will be amazed at the behavior, vocalizations, and care requirements of a bird. I spell out all this information for you in this book.

If you own a cockatiel or plan to get one soon, you need to know that the next 20 years of your life will include cleaning up the mess that birds can make, keeping water dishes clean, quieting screeches, and dining while a cockatiel patters around on the table. Yes, a cockatiel may live to be 20 years old and beyond, barring illness or accidents. So you need to be prepared to accept the fact that cockatiels are messy animals. They eliminate often, keeping themselves light for quick flight, and they can't be housetrained. They throw things, such as food and toys, off the top of their cage for fun or to get your attention. You and the vacuum cleaner will become good friends. Cockatiels may scream and bite you. Twice a year they systematically shed their old feathers and grow shiny new ones. The amount of feathers lost makes you wonder if you aren't caring for an animal three times their size. And you better love chopping and thawing vegetables because fixing a plate of veggies for Sydney will become part of your morning routine. Just consider your bird's food choice an opportunity to change your diet and to become well acquainted with the produce aisle at your local grocery store.

And you know what? You'll probably find that owning a cockatiel is worth all the work and time commitment. Your cleaning time and care can result in one of the most satisfying companion animals you're ever likely to know. When you aspire to bird ownership, you probably imagine a companion bird who likes you. One who will ride on your shoulder, share your life, and appreciate cuddles. One whom your friends will be awed by and can also handle. You imagine a bird who is a good mimic and can get adequate exercise in most apartments or homes.

Cockatiels are parrots, and a cockatiel is the bird most people really want when they think of getting a parrot. They come with many of the requirements of parrot keeping without most of the drawbacks.

With a cockatiel, you get more than you could ever expect. They are common pet birds, with an uncommon ability to steal your heart and to become integral members of your family. Cockatiels love your company and seek it out. They happily accompany you around the house to do mundane chores. They usually like to be cuddled or petted or scratched, and they retain this trait into adulthood. A friendly cockatiel learns to woo your friends and neighbors. It's no accident that most of my friends have cockatiels, even if they didn't have one before they met me and the flock! Cockatiels have the kind of charm and outgoing personality that is not easily contained in a cage. They'll spend a lot of time out of it with the family. You may even end up sharing your pet with broader audiences at a bird club, nursing home, library, or elementary school. And when did that photo of Sydney sneak into your wallet?

Living with Cockatiels

Living with a cockatiel starts at daybreak. Unless you cover a cockatiel's cage to darken his environment, your little squirt will be up with the sun. The first order of business is breakfast. The difference between your breakfast and your cockatiel's breakfast will blur over time. Birds are flock animals, and you're becoming a member of a bird flock by adopting your cockatiel. If you feed your cockatiel in his cage, you'll notice that he will eat at the same time you do. The flock eats together. If your cockatiel is out on your shoulder or on the table, he will eat some of what you're having for breakfast! Be prepared to share food with your new feathered friend. The secret to your cockatiel's happiness is being with you as you go about your daily activities.

Activities suitable for your cockatiel companion to enjoy with you include breakfast, showering, traveling around as you go about your morning routine, working, studying, paying bills, reading, or watching TV. Meals and snacks are favorite cockatiel pastimes. Wild bird watching also can be fun for them. So can tearing up small crunchy objects or rolling around larger, more solid items. You'll find that you're doing less and less of the TV watching mentioned earlier and more watching your cockatiel play and explore. Your junk mail will become playthings and provide entertainment.

Cockatiels are also like potato chips. Sometimes you can't stop after owning one. A cockatiel is that much fun and that lovable! But you need to think long and hard about acquiring more cockatiels or adding additional birds to your household. Each one requires and deserves equal care and attention from you (see Figure 1-1). For example, you need to provide care for all your birds when you're on vacation or away on business. In addition, you'll have the cost of veterinary checkups and new toys and twice (or more?) the dust and feathers to clean up.

Figure 1-1:
Cockatiels
need (and
love)
attention.

Are you adding a second cockatiel to your family? Your current family pet cockatiel may not be as accepting of a newcomer as you expect. Many pet cockatiels think of themselves as a "little person" and love human company. A pet cockatiel may not recognize another cockatiel as his friend and may not welcome him. There can be jealousy between them and rivalry for your attention.

What are you getting yourself into? You're acquiring a companion, a clown, an entertainer, a lovebug, and a small bundle of feathers with a huge heart and ample love to spread in this world. Welcome to the world of cockatiels. I wish you a long and happy association and have compiled in this book all the tips, tricks, information, and advice I can think of to give you a good start. Cockatiel ownership is neither as simple nor as mystifying as you think. It is also more rewarding than you can imagine.

Demystifying Color Mutations

Cockatiels come in many colors and patterns (see Figure 1-2). But I want to make it clear that there is not a big difference in temperament or personality among the different cockatiel color mutations. Whew! That leaves you to make a choice based on your personal preference. Though personality does not vary among colors of cockatiels, it varies greatly among individual birds for reasons that have nothing to do with color. Any color cockatiel may be excessively inbred, may be well bred, or may come from an aviary that produces healthy or sickly birds. Color is a minor consideration compared to health and personality. But it's still a factor to consider. I'm sure you want to know what the color mutations look like and what they're called.

You should be color-blind when choosing your companion cockatiel. The best cockatiel for you is the one with a personality that is compatible with you and your lifestyle. Cockatiels can be demanding, noisy, submissive, calm, curious, playful, jokesters, aggressive, broody, outgoing, affectionate, or introverted — and more. You'll face more personality choices than color choices when choosing your bird!

Normal gray cockatiels

Cockatiels in the wild are gray birds. Some cockatiels in captivity are also basically gray birds (see Figure 1-2). They sport a white wing patch and a bright orange-red cheek patch, and the mature males have yellow heads. Gray cockatiels are more than "basic gray." They have the right accessories for the makings of a beautiful bird. Because gray is the normal or natural color for a cockatiel, many of our companion gray cockatiels also carry genetics for color patterns or genetics to have different color offspring. When a breeding pair of cockatiels is different colors, or when one color is dominant, the bird's color defaults to the wild gray color.

Cockatiels are special among the parrot species because you can tell the sexes apart when they're over 6 months old. At that time, cockatiels go through their first *molt,* or systematic shedding of feathers, replacing them with new ones. Female gray cockatiels retain the coloring they had as babies. They have bars underneath their tail feathers and show only a hint of yellow on their face at the forehead or jowls. Males explode into their flashier coloring at this age. Their head becomes a vibrant yellow, and the feathers under their tail become solid black. Gray cockatiels range from light to dark in color, with no special names for the shades of gray.

Pattern mutations in cockatiels: Pied and pearl

Some cockatiel mutations affect the patterning of color on a cockatiel's feathers (see Figure 1-2). These mutations are the pearl and pied mutations. Normal or wild-colored gray cockatiels are one solid color except for their white wing patches. Pied cockatiels vary greatly in their overall appearance. But pied cockatiels do have one trait in common with each other: They all have patches of color on their body and other patches of white-to-yellow light coloring. For the sake of convenience, I'm going to call the non-colored feathers "white," but they do range from bright white to yellow. The colored part of a pied can be any color. You'll see gray pied, cinnamon pied, and silver pied cockatiels. The patches of light and dark on a cockatiel can be distributed in any number of ways. A dark cockatiel with a few white feathers in his crest or a white tail feather is a pied cockatiel. Occasionally, an all-white cockatiel with dark eyes appears, making it technically a pied bird, except that nature forgot his darker feathers. If a white cockatiel has one dark feather, he is a pied cockatiel. Markings are often relatively balanced and symmetrical, with the most dark markings on a bird's wings and maybe a band across his chest.

Hybrid versus mutation

The terms "hybrid" and "mutation" are sometimes confused. A hybrid is a cross between two different species. Hybrid birds occur in the macaws, such as breedings between the pure species scarlet macaw, blue-and-gold macaw, and green-winged macaw. Other hybrid birds include crosses between sun, nanday, and/or Jjnday conures. Beautiful apricot and red-tinged canaries are descendents of hybrid birds that are crosses between domestic canaries and the black-hooded red siskin.

Mutations occur naturally in one species and affect the color or other physical traits of a bird.

The colors found in cockatiels are all mutations that have been developed in captivity since the 1940s. Selective breeding and inbreeding that would not occur in the wild have accelerated the development of cockatiel mutations in captivity. Cockatiels, no matter what their color, are still cockatiels; they aren't a mix of species. Cockatiels in the wild are gray birds. Hence the use of the term "normal gray" for these birds in our domestic flocks.

Figure 1-2:
Some cockatiels with interesting color patterns.

Some breeders who specialize in exhibition cockatiels try to breed white birds with small, even, and symmetrical patches of colors at the top of the wings. Color on the face is termed a "dirty face" and is less than ideal. The head, flight feathers, chest, and tail are all white. Cockatiels such as these, who are mainly white with some color, are termed "heavy pied." Cockatiels who are pied but are mainly a dark color are called "light pied." You may never need to know this term, but if you ever hear it, you'll know that people aren't talking about a bird's weight or the springiness of his step.

The only color mutation where you can't tell the girls from the boys is the pied mutation. You have to rely upon behavioral clues to tell you your bird's sex. By 3 or 4 months old, male cockatiels usually learn the wolf whistle and may start to strut or hop to show off to the girls (or their reflection in a mirror, or you!). Girls remain quiet. If you really need to know a cockatiel's sex, a DNA blood test can help determine it. Ask your cockatiel's veterinarian to do the test for you.

When a pied cockatiel is a member of a pair of cockatiels and it's mate is not pied or is not carrying the recessive gene for pied-ness, some interesting markings result. Because pied is a recessive mutation, it is passed along to cockatiel chicks of both sexes of such a pair. Most genetic codes are pretty invisible to cockatiel breeders, and it's not obvious by color or markings what sort of genes a cockatiel is carrying. When a cockatiel is "split pied," however, or carries the recessive gene to have pied chicks itself, he may have "pied" markings on its body. Usually such a marking is a fleck of yellow on the back of the head or at the nape. A cockatiel carrying the recessive gene to produce pied chicks may itself have a two-toned beak, or pied feet. Now you don't have to wonder why your cockatiel may have a stray mark on it.

Pearl cockatiels have an attractive all-over pattern. Usually the pearl bird is a solid color, which may be gray, cinnamon, lutino (white to creamy yellow), or any of the other cockatiel colors. Each feather on his body is edged with yellow or creamy white. The head and tail are also yellow or white. The lacy pattern is very attractive, but if a pearl is a male, he will lose this patterning, beginning at his first molt at about 6 months of age. Eventually, over the next two years, the males become solid-colored birds and are indistinguishable from other solid-colored males. They are still pearls and will have pearl chicks, making records and ID bands very important for breeders of these lovely cockatiels! If you have an adult pearl cockatiel, you will know its sex. If you like the pearl pattern, plan to get a female bird so you can enjoy it, or be ready for a big change if you get a male or don't know the sex of your chick.

Solid color mutations in cockatiels

In addition to pattern mutations, color mutations have also appeared in cockatiels.

Lutino cockatiels

One of the truly striking color mutations in cockatiels is lutino, white cockatiels with hints of buttery yellow and a bright crimson cheek patch. As chicks, lutino cockatiels have red eyes, but as adults, their eyes can look quite dark. Though this bird is light in color, he is not an albino.

Albino cockatiels are true albinos. They lack pigment in their eyes, feathers, beaks, and feet. They have no cheek patch, and their feathers are bright white. Technically, however, they are a double mutation. The correct term for an albino cockatiel is a *whiteface-lutino*.

Even though lutino cockatiels are white, they still show light markings that allow you to know the sex of the birds once they've attained their adult feathering after 6 months of age. Look at the underside of a female's tail, and you will see light white and yellow striping in the same pattern that shows up as yellow and black in a normal gray cockatiel. Check out your bird in very bright light, as the coloring is faint. A male has solid color white or yellowish feathers under his tail, with no striping whatsoever.

Patterns in cockatiel feathering can, similarly, appear in lutinos. The lutino-pearl mutation is subtly beautiful. The yellow lacing on the body gives this bird a buttery yellow coloring. Of course, as with normal pearl cockatiels, males lose this lacing and look like a normal lutino. Lutino-pied cockatiels have blocks of yellow on them. These birds are difficult to distinguish from a regular lutino cockatiel.

Lutino cockatiels may have health problems. They often have a large bald spot on their head, behind their crest. They may have more frequent night frights than other color mutations and also have more problems with breaking blood feathers after such incidents. For more on blood feathers, read "The molting process" in Chapter 9. If you are attracted to this mutation, choose your cockatiel carefully from someone breeding selectively to produce stable, healthy birds. The wisest breeders do not breed lutinos together in pairs but cross their lutino birds with another mutation.

Cinnamon cockatiels

Another mutation color for cockatiels is cinnamon. As you can tell by the name, this mutation is toasty brown. A bird of this color really looks just like a normal gray cockatiel, except that where a gray is gray, a cinnamon cockatiel is brown. The males have yellow heads, and the females have yellow and cinnamon stripes under their tails. Sometimes cinnamon birds develop a mottled appearance called marbling, with blotches of lighter coloring in their feathers. I've never heard a satisfactory explanation for this occurrence. Perhaps it results from fading in sunlight? What's important for you is to know that it is normal and no cause for alarm.

Color and pattern combinations

Cockatiel colors and patterns can combine. Cinnamon-pied and cinnamon-pearl are especially nice color and pattern combinations. They can all combine together, even. Isn't genetics fun? The cinnamon-pearl-pied cockatiel is a pretty mutation with blocks of white and color on its body. The colored part is cinnamon, with a pearl pattern in it. Gorgeous!

But as creative as cockatiel mutations can get, some mutations just don't go together very well. For example, in the cinnamon-lutino cockatiel, which is a double mutation on paper, lutino masks cinnamon, and the bird usually looks like a lutino. A cinnamon-lutino bird may even have a faint brown wash on light feathers; it looks like neither one color nor the other. It's not a desirable color combination.

Whiteface cockatiels

The whiteface mutation in cockatiels has a couple striking characteristics. This mutation suppresses all traces of yellow in a cockatiel's coloring. The result is a cockatiel that looks like a living black-and-white photo. Lacking is the red cheek patch characteristic of cockatiels of other colors. Male whiteface cockatiels have a white head by the time they're mature, whereas a normal or cinnamon male has a yellow head. Female whiteface cockatiels are gray, and the stripes under their tail are white and black instead of yellow and black.

The whiteface cockatiel coloring has been combined with other cockatiel feather patterns and colors through the work of diligent breeders and the wonder of genetics. This means that besides the generic whiteface cockatiel, you can find whiteface pearl and whiteface pied cockatiels and whiteface-pearl-pied cockatiels. What's more, there are cinnamon whiteface-pearl-pied cockatiels, cinnamon-whiteface-pearl, and cinnamon-whiteface-pied among the possibilities. Breeders call these double, triple, and quadruple mutations.

What happens when the whiteface mutation, with no yellow, is combined with the lutino mutation, with no gray color on a cockatiel? This is when the albino appears in nests! Albino is not a separate color mutation in cockatiels but is a double mutation, a combination of both the whiteface and lutino mutations.

Avid breeders and cockatiel exhibitors raise cockatiels in other color mutations, though they're seldom available as companion cockatiels. They are rarer than the other mutations I list earlier, but they can be found!

The fallow cockatiel looks like a soft brown cinnamon cockatiel, but he is suffused with yellow, and his eyes are red. Both dominant and recessive silver cockatiels are silver-gray birds. Recessive silvers have red eyes. The pastel and yellowface cockatiel mutations are differentiated by their cheek patches. The pastel has a very light peach cheek patch, and a yellowface has a yellow cheek patch. All of these more unusual mutations combine with the other mutation colors and patterns.

The important thing about cockatiel color mutations is that they aren't important. Simply realize that you have many choices and then pick out a cockatiel that is pleasing to you. If you choose a cockatiel based on his health and personality and obtain him from a reliable source, you'll come to love whatever color bird that is! You'll spend most of your time gazing into those inquisitive eyes, anyway.

Cockatiel Misconceptions

A little birdy may have told you something about what it's like to have a companion cockatiel. If your source is a cockatiel owner with a relationship with his bird, there is probably some truth to their statements. On the other hand, many bird care myths are circulating among the general population. These are some of the things you may have heard about cockatiel ownership:

> ✔ Birds are easy to care for.
>
> ✔ Cockatiels are easy to breed.
>
> ✔ You already know how to care for a pet.
>
> ✔ Cockatiels don't hold food with their feet.
>
> ✔ It's cruel to clip a bird's wings.
>
> ✔ Any parrot talks.

Birds are easy to care for

That heading may not be not good grammar (the statement ends in a preposition), but you get the gist. Birds may *seem* easy to care for. You feed and water a bird and keep him in its cage, right? If only it were so simple. The fact that a cockatiel is a caged pet means that you must supply more that just the basic needs — including anything the bird would find in nature or by being a member of a flock. You are the sun and rain, the source of forage and safety and water, and the companionship for your cockatiel. Birds are small animals with extensive respiratory systems. They are easily affected by the growth of mold or bacteria, so their environment must be kept clean — by you. Cockatiels need to be bathed regularly — by you — to keep the shiny quality of their feathers. Besides a formulated diet, cockatiels need supplemental vegetables in their diet and appreciate fun snacks — which you prepare and offer. Cockatiels are flock animals. They expect to eat, have fun, and play with and interact with flockmates. That's you, again.

Cockatiels are easy to breed

We wouldn't have any companion birds if they didn't breed in captivity. We especially wouldn't have cockatiels, who can't be exported from Australia. Does this statement mean that a cockatiel is a beginner bird so you can learn to breed and hand-feed birds? Perhaps. The best cockatiels are raised by someone who loves and respects cockatiels for the outstanding small parrots they are, however. Such people have a commitment to cockatiel owners and to the birds themselves. They aren't just practicing for "the real thing." Cockatiels *are* the real thing; they're small parrots who respond to the same care and attention we give any parrot. I hope you appreciate the attention, time, and care given to your chick by some hardworking cockatiel breeder. When cockatiels hatch, they are blind, covered with down, and the size of a bumblebee. Six weeks later, they have feathers and look like cockatiels. During those six weeks, breeders must take care of lots of feedings and cage cleaning and give the birds plenty of attention. It's a wonder breeders can ever part with their babies.

Since the Wild Bird Conservation Act of October 1995, importing most parrot species into the United States has been illegal. The exception is some mutation colors of parrots that have obviously been bred in captivity. Without unrelated parrots from wild populations, the gene pool from which to raise parrot chicks is limited to the birds that have come to the U.S. prior to 1995. Australia has banned the export of its wildlife (which includes cockatiels) since the 1940s. Luckily, cockatiels are well established in the aviculturual community — those people who keep and breed birds in captivity.

You already know how to care for a pet

A cockatiel may not be your first pet. Perhaps you've had a dog or cat, a hamster, or a pony. Even so, don't assume that you know anything about bird care, except that he requires love. Birds are special creatures with special care requirements. Read all you can about bird care. (By the way, thanks for picking up this book and reading it! Obviously, you have a clue that you need an understanding of cockatiels to live with one and care for him properly.) Talk to other bird owners. By finding out all you can about your bird, you and your cockatiel are off to a fantastic start.

Cockatiels don't hold food with their feet

The statement that cockatiels don't hold food with their feet is included in many other books and articles about cockatiels. It's supposed to be one of the differences between cockatiels and true parrots. It just isn't true in real life, however. Some, though not all, cockatiels pick food up with their feet to eat it. By the way, many birds are left-footed. Of course, there are some "northpaws" out there in cockatieldom, as well. I've noticed that some families of cockatiels tend to like to hold food and other cockatiels show no inclination to do so.

It's cruel to clip a bird's wings

Keeping your companion animal safe from harm is never cruel. The actual action of clipping a bird's wings is similar to clipping a person's fingernails. Grown feathers have no nerves or feeling in them. Clipping a bird's wings is a way to slow a cockatiel down in a home environment. Cockatiels are built aerodynamically, and they're swift flyers. When a cockatiel crashes into a window or mirror at full tilt, the result can be deadly. Proper wing clipping lessens this possibility. It's painless, and clipped wing feathers do grow back. There is a longer explanation of wing clipping in Chapter 6.

Clipped wings on cockatiels and other parrots grow back with each molt. Some birds, usually waterfowl, are permanently grounded by pinioning, which is the removal of the outer wing bone so that the bird can never fly. Clipping a bird's wings is simply a temporary way to slow his flight. Clipped feathers regrow at the bird's next molt.

Though you can learn to clip a bird's wing feathers yourself, it's probably a good idea to have an expert show you the first time. That way, the clipper can point out blood feathers and the correct clipping pattern. The following people can help:

- ✔ Avian veterinarian
- ✔ Bird groomer
- ✔ Bird shop staff
- ✔ Cockatiel breeder
- ✔ Experienced cockatiel pet owner

When restraining a cockatiel, don't compress his chest, as doing so prevents the bird from breathing. Check for blood feathers before clipping a cockatiel's wings. Injury to a blood feather results in pain and blood loss for your bird. Learn to clip wings from an experienced wing clipper or schedule an appointment with an expert for your bird's wing clipping needs. I cover the tasks of clipping wings and trimming nails in Chapter 6.

Any parrot talks

Oh, yeah? This statement is meant to make you look at your priorities in bird ownership. Many parrots talk, and most parrots can talk to some degree. A cockatiel is not one of those birds well known for talking ability. Many don't learn words. Of these, most are males. Males usually can learn a variety of whistles. You have plenty of other reasons to treasure your companion cockatiel. If you're absolutely certain that you want a talking bird, a cockatiel is probably not for you. Just warning you!

What Makes Birds Different from Other Pets?

There are obvious physical differences between the most common companion animals — dogs and cats — and our companion birds. Both dogs and cats have fur. Birds have feathers. Dogs and cats have eyes that both face forward, indicative of a predator. Our cockatiels and other parrots have eyes on either side of their head. The predatory birds such as owls and eagles have forward-facing eyes. Parrots are much more brightly colored than dogs and cats, with cockatiels sporting some of those bright colors. Birds can fly; dogs and cats cannot. Anything else? Birds can talk, whereas our other companions do not.

Our companion birds are prey animals, and the most common companion animals we keep in our homes are dogs and cats, both predatory animals. Prey animals such as cockatiels and other parrots have different sets of important senses. Dogs and cats rely a great deal on their sense of smell to hunt prey. A dog becomes comfortable around you after being able to smell you. We can only imagine what it's like to have such a heightened sense of smell. Birds such as cockatiels, on the other hand, have little olfactory capability.

Cockatiels rely on their keen eyesight to catch sight of predators coming upon them from many angles. Notice that your cockatiel watches you closely and that your actions are important to him. Your bird will be observant about objects that are quite far away and objects in his environment that are new or unusual as well. A cockatiel also can see colors. Dogs and cats see only some colors, and much of their world is shades of gray. Birds see colors, wear colorful feathers to show off for each other, and appreciate colors in their environment.

Dogs and cats have very physical relationships with each other. But cockatiels don't wrestle and tumble around a whole lot with each other. They need every bone, every appendage, and every feather on their bodies to be in perfect condition so that they can stay safe. Working with a cockatiel regarding behavior, discipline, and training then becomes an intellectual exercise. Though this approach is different in many ways from how we work with companion dogs, it has something in common with working with horses. Horses are also prey animals. We cannot control them physically because of their size, but we develop trust relationships and intellectual relationships that work for both the animal and the human involved.

Cockatiels are more apt than most companion dogs and cats to be kept in cages. A caged animal is completely dependent on us for all his needs. That's the responsibility you take on when you adopt your new cockatiel. Cockatiels are also flock animals. They are safest from predators when they travel in groups. They are programmed to belong with a flock and to act and verbalize like their flock. If you understand this, you have the key for getting along with your cockatiel, understanding your actions, and changing behaviors when appropriate. Not only do you need to provide a caged animal with sustenance and a clean environment, but you also must provide or serve as his entertainment. Your cockatiel will learn to enjoy the time he spends with you, his adopted flock.

As a flock animal, your cockatiel will often become part of the flock by doing what you do. Time for dinner? Cheeps will be at her seed dish, too. When your cockatiel can see you grooming, brushing your hair, or putting on makeup, he may take that moment to preen. When music or a television is blaring, your cockatiel will make every attempt to match your din decibel for decibel.

Cockatiels differ from companion dogs in that they don't have an intense desire to please. You will not find that your cockatiel will do something you ask just to make you happy. Instead, the cockatiel and other parrots are the princesses among our companion animals. They do what works for them, to get what they want. What they usually want is pretty basic. Cockatiels want good things to eat, your company, and showers. They're very good at training their people to provide these needs for them.

Companion birds also differ from companion dogs and cats in that there is a wide choice of species for companions. Each species is adapted to a different natural environment and has specific care requirements. There are many breeds of dogs and cats, but there is only one species we keep as domestic animals. Most of them have been domesticated for many generations and bear little resemblance to their wild cousins, the wolf and wild cats.

What Makes Cockatiels Different from Other Pet Birds?

Cockatiels have characteristics that distinguish them from other companion parrots. They're generally good-natured birds. They keep this temperament for their whole lives, even through that difficult adolescent period! Cockatiels can even be both a family pet and a "breeder" bird without losing their tameness. Cockatiels are hardy birds. They're natives of the desert, equipped to survive in harsh conditions. They're not adapted to the abundant food sources of rain forest species. The cockatiel is not an endangered species or in any way rare. Generations of cockatiels have been bred successfully in captivity. Your cockatiel is not needed for the cockatiel gene pool or for potential release to the wild.

In fact, among parrots, the cockatiel is one of the few you could call domesticated. Cockatiels come in colors not found in the wild, and their shape is often different from wild cockatiels. They have successfully bred in captivity for generations, and the cockatiels that are now our companions are often ideally suited to life in our living rooms rather than the Australian bush.

Chapter 2

Choosing Your Own Cockatiel

*W*hen the time is right, you'll make a decision to get a cockatiel. She may be your first pet or your first bird, or she may be an addition to your feathered household. Somehow you were smitten and know that a cockatiel is the companion bird for you. Then you need to decide how you are going to choose your cockatiel. You have many options. The age, tameness, and health of your new cockatiel make a big difference in how happy you are with your new pet.

It will be best for both you and your cockatiel if you make a commitment to your bird. Do your best to get the color and temperament of cockatiel you prefer. Then, when through no fault of the cockatiel she has behaviors that don't meet your expectation, work with her quirks and change your behavior or the bird's environment so that peace is reestablished in the household. Most cockatiels are gentle souls, but maybe you'll get one who communicates by biting, or one who enjoys your company so much that she screams for your attention. You may have wanted a talking or whistling bird, and could instead end up with a female. Maybe you need to get an older bird with mature feathering who already shows a penchant for learning whistles.

Cockatiels Don't Grow on Trees

You have many options when shopping for a cockatiel. You can buy from a cockatiel breeder who breeds a pair or two at home, a breeder with champion exhibition birds, or a breeder with aviaries of cockatiels and all kinds of other birds. You may decide to get your bird from friends who are looking for a new home for their companion cockatiel because of lifestyle changes. You may find your cockatiel in a pet store or local animal shelter or through bird adoption programs. Newspaper classified ads are another source of cockatiels. Cockatiels are available as chicks, as weaned birds, and as older adults. You need to review your needs and to judge the suitability for you of a cockatiel who will become part of your family.

Don't be tempted to buy an unweaned cockatiel chick as your companion bird. Such a bird may be offered less expensively by unscrupulous breeders or stores. A bird does not bond to you more closely because you feed her as a chick. She bonds to the flock that she grows to trust after she is on her own. Weaning is probably the most difficult period in a cockatiel's life, a time when she should be watched over by experienced avian caregivers. They can watch for subtle signs that mean the chick is in trouble. Even veteran hand feeders make mistakes that result in injury or death to growing chicks. Don't try weaning and don't even support this practice. If a breeder or store sells unweaned chicks to inexperienced pet owners, don't spend your dollars there. I'm off my soapbox now.

No matter where you get your cockatiel, your concerns should include the cockatiel's health and your access to coaching about cockatiel ownership. A cockatiel's sex, color, and personality are important issues. I urge you to have an open mind about these cockatiel attributes. More than one cockatiel has picked her new owner herself. There's no explaining chemistry between a bird and a human being.

You need to be aware of some basic conditions that should be present wherever you obtain your cockatiel (see Figure 2-1). The location should be clean, and the birds should look healthy and cared for. The facility or breeder should guarantee the health of your new bird. In the case of a rescue or adoption organization, it probably can't guarantee a bird's health, so you should be willing to pay any veterinary bills required to get your cockatiel into good health. A cockatiel seller should also be willing to help you set up your new cockatiel comfortably. The seller should supply you with information and access to sources of information such as books and publications. The seller should also be willing to answer your questions over the first few days and weeks (and maybe even years!) you have your cockatiel.

The very best way to find a source for your own companion cockatiel is through a referral. Ideally, a referral comes from someone who has a happy, healthy cockatiel of her own or from someone who deals professionally with the breeders, agencies, and stores in your area. Such a professional might be an avian veterinarian or a pet store owner who doesn't sell live animals but knows the local breeders. Another source of referrals is bird club members, who probably know suppliers of happy, healthy cockatiels in your area.

Figure 2-1:
Gather as
much
information
as you can
before
choosing a
cockatiel.

Using a bird breeder

If I had to recommend one place to get a companion cockatiel, it would be a local breeder who cares a great deal about cockatiels and knows the birds individually. Simply being a cockatiel breeder isn't good enough, however. A breeder should meet exacting criteria and should be recommended to you by a satisfied customer or avian professional. Use your own judgment about the cleanliness of a breeder's home or aviary and how willing the breeder is to help you learn more about your new companion cockatiel.

If a bird breeder talks to you about having a *closed flock,* that's a good sign. This avicultural term means that the breeder has tested her birds for illness and doesn't introduce new birds to the flock without strict quarantine. Don't be surprised if you aren't welcome near breeding birds. You may disturb the birds who are diligent about their parenting duties. In the eyes of a concerned breeder, you may carry disease on your clothes from visits to other bird facilities or pet stores.

Bird breeders are individuals who vary in method and scale. Here are a few examples:

✔ **Hobby breeders:** Don't earn a living breeding birds. They earn extra money or breed birds for the love of birds or to satisfy their own nurturing instincts. These breeders convert living rooms, garages, and spare bedrooms to space for breeding.

✔ **Cockatiel exhibitors:** Breed birds with a standard in mind, hoping for top prizes at bird shows. Exhibitors usually show birds they have raised themselves. Not all cockatiels they produce meet their criteria for exhibiting and for breeding, so companion cockatiels are available from them. Exhibitors are often interested in breeding the rarest mutation colors in cockatiels.

✔ **Aviaries and farms:** Some breeders with aviaries or flights of cockatiels may still not breed birds as their main income. They may sell to the public or may sell larger quantities of birds to pet stores. A larger-scale breeder may hire others to hand-feed chicks.

✔ **Commercial breeders:** The largest scale of breeder is the commercial breeder, who breeds large quantities of birds to meet the needs of the pet trade. Breeding birds is their business — it's how they earn their income. You will probably never buy a single pet from one of these facilities directly. You may buy a commercially-bred cockatiel at a pet store.

You should be able to get a young cockatiel from a breeder who should offer a health guarantee for your new chick. Find out whether the breeder is willing to trim your cockatiel's wings when they grow out, or ask the breeder who she recommends for this job. Bird breeders are busy people. They have a lot of mouths to feed and often do their job overnight, when they're caring for newly hatched chicks. The best way to stay on their good side is to keep your appointment with a bird breeder, call at the designated hours, and get the information you need without wasting time. The best way to get on the bad side of a knowledgeable bird breeder is to buy a bird somewhere else and then call the breeder to ask for help or information about caring for it! My conservative estimate is that every buyer and prospective buyer takes two hours of a breeder's time. A breeder discusses bird care, feeding, wing clipping, and a bird's history and may show you the bird's parents. The breeder will also ask about your reason for wanting a cockatiel, how you will house her, and what your family and lifestyle are like.

The reason a bird breeder is so snoopy about you is that she has nurtured this little cockatiel baby from a hatchling who looks like a fuzzy bumble bee. She has watched the bird grow into a lumpy baby with pinfeathers and has stayed up late and gotten up early to keep it fed and happy. Finally, in an ugly duckling-like transformation, a gangly chick ends up with real feathers and learns coordination and cockatiel skills. You have no idea how attached breeders are to their babies. Rely on this attachment if you're looking for particular traits in your new baby. Cockatiel chicks exhibit different personalities at a young age. A cockatiel breeder often notices which of the chicks is friendly, shy, talkative, or passive and can help match you with an appropriate chick — if the breeder lets you have one! Breeders have a difficult time letting their babies go. As a cockatiel breeder, I always wonder whether my chicks will receive the love and care they need and deserve when they go to a new home.

Going to the pet store: How much is that cockatiel in the window?

Just as there are exemplary bird breeders, there are also excellent pet stores. Many buy hand-feeding baby cockatiels from a reputable breeder and finish feeding and socializing the chicks. They may also buy weaned chicks to sell, again from a source they trust. An excellent pet store won't sell you a chick until she has indeed weaned, however. As with any source of cockatiels, look for a clean environment, a health guarantee, and assistance with your cockatiel after the sale.

Sometimes pet stores get a bad rap. There are some pet stores and breeders that I could not recommend as a source for a cockatiel. You can find some good pet stores, however. Search for one of those and get a recommendation. You can get every bit as good a companion cockatiel as you would from a private breeder. Pet stores have their place in the business of aviculture. Not every breeder has sales and marketing skills or will spend the time required with each customer buying a single cockatiel. For these people, who may be brilliant at caring for adult cockatiels and breeding them, a pet store offers an outlet for their chicks. After all, they're in business. In turn, concerned pet store personnel often have the sales and people skills needed to match birds and owners. They also know that a caring bird owner will be back on a monthly if not a weekly basis to keep her bird supplied with food, toys, and treats.

A pet store may also offer other useful services. The staff may trim wings, groom your bird, or even board birds. Eventually, you may want to take a vacation and leave your cockatiel behind, as much as you'll enjoy your time with it in the beginning. Some stores also offer educational opportunities. They may offer bird care classes or sponsor an occasional seminar. If they don't offer this live training, they may rent educational videos or show them in the store. Of course, they're out shopping for the latest in toys and accessories for your bird, so stay in touch if you find a good pet store.

If a pet store in your community keeps its animals in dirty, cramped conditions and the birds do not look well cared for, stay far away. Stressed birds are more likely to carry disease, and you can take home many of the major bird diseases on your clothes and shoes.

Visiting a bird rescue or adoption center

Cockatiels often find homes through adoption centers for birds or through adoption programs run by bird clubs. Birds also are available occasionally at your local animal shelter. Unfortunately, there is a need for bird rescue and adoption. This need will only grow as our long-lived pets transition between homes and as people continue to breed cockatiels indiscriminately.

If you're looking for a cockatiel as a pet, a cockatiel is probably available who needs a home. They are often older cockatiels, not chicks. Sometimes they were found outdoors, having escaped from their home or aviary. I hope you'll take the hint and keep your companion's wings safely trimmed. An adopted cockatiel is of unknown age, but you may know its sex and temperament. That's more than you usually know when buying a cockatiel chick under 6 months of age. If the cockatiel you adopt is friendly and hand tame, or knows a repertoire of whistles, or speaks a few words, you don't have to guess about its abilities. It is possible to tame and train an older cockatiel who is shy or scared. Be aware that this a much more lengthy process than you will have with a chick or a cockatiel who is tame but needs to adjust to your home.

You will probably get no guarantee of health or breeding when you adopt a cockatiel. Be sure to plan a vet visit for your adopted cockatiel and figure that expense into the cost of the bird. Adopting a cockatiel through a rescue group or adoption center isn't necessarily the least expensive way to get a new pet, though you can feel good about providing a home for a cockatiel in need.

Adopting a companion cockatiel from a bird placement program or a bird club may not be as easy as you might imagine. You probably will have to fill out forms regarding your lifestyle and knowledge of bird care. (Good thing you're reading this book! You'll look good when you fill out those forms.) The adoption program will probably ask you questions about the number of birds in your home, how you plan to house your new cockatiel, and what you know about bird care and feeding. The adoption program will certainly ask you whether you have other cockatiels and whether you breed birds or plan to. Many placement programs don't want to place their birds in situations that will breed more unwanted birds.

If you plan to breed cockatiels, you probably won't be able to adopt a companion cockatiel from bird adoption or rescue organizations. They don't want to be responsible for procreation that leads to more unwanted birds!

You may be tempted to "rescue" a cockatiel yourself from a pet store or breeder where you feel it is being mistreated. Stop and consider for a moment that where you buy your cockatiel is a vote for that business, making it possible for the store or breeder to stay in business. What do you want to support? Buy your cockatiel from someone taking exceptional care of her birds, or from a well-organized rescue or adoption program that makes a difference in your community and has actions consistent with its values. If you are unhappy with the care a facility gives its birds, talk to the management. Lack of food or water can be reported to a humane society.

The Health Guarantee

Reputable breeders and stores should offer you a written guarantee that your new cockatiel is healthy. Most such guarantees are valid for a few days, giving you time to take the cockatiel to see a bird veterinarian at your own expense. If someone isn't willing to give you a written guarantee of health, I recommend that you not deal with the seller. Even though you probably feel all warm and fuzzy about your companion cockatiel and plan for her to be your lifelong friend, the business of selling cockatiels is still a business. Is there anything you purchase that you would not want to return if it were defective? Don't you feel best working with businesses that stand behind their products?

The exact nature of your guarantee will vary. A guarantee may specify that you get your money back, that you may exchange your cockatiel for another, or that the seller will pay for the veterinary care required to make your cockatiel well again. Talk the options over with your veterinarian as well as the breeder. Two conditions that are fairly common in cockatiel chicks, bacterial infections and yeast infections, are also easily treatable. It may not be cost effective to the seller, or emotionally gratifying to you, to treat more-serious conditions.

The relatively short period for which most cockatiels are guaranteed by their sellers is a reflection of the way in which avian diseases are transmitted. A seller cannot control your actions. If you introduce your cockatiel to other birds in your home, she could contract a condition they have or carry. Many bird diseases are airborne, and you can unwittingly transmit illness to your companion birds after visiting a bird fair or a pet shop with birds.

The more informal cockatiel sellers may not offer a health guarantee. Such sellers include private individuals selling or giving away family pets, animal shelters, and bird adoption programs. In these cases, you knowingly take the responsibility for any health care the cockatiel may need. And you should have its health status checked! Sometimes buying a cockatiel this way works out just fine, and other times a "good deal" proves to be much more expensive than buying a quality cockatiel from a reputable source.

Acquiring a Used Pet

I am an advocate of the "used" pet cockatiel as a companion. These cockatiels come to you as adults, and slightly used, which hopefully means tame or talking! Used cockatiels come from various sources in various conditions. They may have been well cared for, or barely cared for. They may need a new home because they have learned bad habits or because their owner is going through a life transition. A used cockatiel may be available for free, or you may pay as much for it as for a chick. It also may come with or without a cage. Here are some sources of used cockatiels:

- ✔ Bird club members
- ✔ Classified ads

 ✔ Coworkers

 ✔ Family

 ✔ Friends

 ✔ Neighbors

Used cockatiels come with the lowest initial price tags, or may even be gifts to you. They also come in all states of health and tameness. You assume the responsibility for the cockatiel's health. Consider an appointment with an avian veterinarian as part of the cost of your new cockatiel. Don't be tempted to forgo this health check-up, either. Cockatiels, as all parrots, are prey animals in the wild. Their life depends on their ability to appear healthy and keep up with their flock so that they don't become dinner for a predator. Only lab tests will tell you how healthy your new cockatiels is; you can't rely on a visual inspection or an assurance by the past owner that she's never needed to take the bird to a veterinarian for an illness.

As with any cockatiel from a private party, you probably won't receive a guarantee of a cockatiel's health or your satisfaction with the bird. This kind of cockatiel adoption is similar to the used vehicles you buy "as is" on a car lot. You make a commitment and deal with the consequences. You'll have the happiest experience if you get a cockatiel that has been living with a loving family and has had regular veterinary care. Some cockatiels whose families don't understand them , or who have moved on to other interests, really bloom with their new owners, where they finally get care, attention, and socialization.

Calculating the Costs

There's nothing wrong with hopping around and finding the best deal for your cockatiel purchase. You need to evaluate what is really a deal for you when it comes to cockatiels. A "free" bird never really is because you must take it to the veterinarian. If you're lucky, the bird is healthy, and you got a good deal. If you're "fixing" a health problem caused by a poor environment, stress, or a poor diet, the bird can get costly very fast. In Table 2-1, I estimate the costs of cockatiels and accessories from different sources. I assume that you'll get a cockatiel from a breeder or pet store only if it comes with a health guarantee. I also assume that you'll provide an adopted cockatiel with the health care she requires.

Table 2-1	The Varying Costs of a Cockatiel Purchase			
Purchase	*Breeder or Pet Store*	*Classifieds*	*Used Pet A*	*Used Pet B*
Cockatiel	$130	$75	$30	$0
Cage/stand	$110	$25	$25	$0
Vet check	$80	$80	$80	$80
Treatment	$0	$35	$250	$0
Totals	$320	$215	$385	$80

Add the cost of feed, veggies, toys, dishes, and a cuttlebone to the costs in the table. These are hypothetical prices, which need to be adjusted for your area. Your local cockatiels may be more or less expensive, as may your veterinary fees. On a yearly basis, add the cost of a bird sitter or other arrangements that allow you to take a vacation.

Part-time cockatiels

If your lifestyle is extremely busy, or if you still aren't sure that a cockatiel is the right bird for you, consider a part-time cockatiel. There is a big need for qualified pet-sitters for birds. Birds have different needs than dogs and cats and require caretakers who understand them. Through an association with a breeder, a bird club, or a parrot adoption organization, you can probably arrange to learn more about birds and to care for birds while owners are on vacation. Adoption centers often need foster homes for birds until they're adopted. Cockatiel-sitting is a way for you to "try on" many species or many cockatiels, getting to know the quirks of males, females, tame, and untame cockatiels, as well as different species of birds.

You can arrange to have a part-time cockatiel through friends, or you may have a more businesslike arrangement, such as pet sitting. Classroom birds often need summer lodging.

Your obligation is to ask a lot of questions about the individual bird, find out what you need to provide for her, and how the real owners handle behavior issues with that bird, if there are any. You'll learn after caring for only a few cockatiels that individual birds vary greatly in personality. Finding a bird that fits your personality and lifestyle will make a lot of sense after you've tested the waters a bit by caring for a variety of cockatiels.

If you have a lifestyle that involves frequent trips, bird-sitting may be a long-term solution to having birds in your life. Birds require daily care and quite a bit of socialization. If you can offer that for days or weeks at a time, but don't know about years at a time, think about this solution to cockatiel ownership. It's a win-win situation for both if you find someone who needs occasional or regular care for a cockatiel or if you can offer a foster bird a refuge.

Questions to Ask When You're Cockatiel Shopping

The answers to the following questions can help you determine whether you're obtaining the right cockatiel from the right person.

Do you offer a health guarantee with this cockatiel?

This question is extremely important. A breeder or pet store should stand behind its product. Go on to another location if the answer is "no" from one of those sources. Adoption programs and private sellers probably won't offer a guarantee. You're taking your chances.

How old is this cockatiel?

This question isn't necessarily important to the quality of pet you get, but you'll want to know. Your companion cockatiel should be weaned, so it shouldn't be younger than 6 weeks old. It is very likely that the youngest cockatiels available to you will be 8 to 10 weeks old. When a cockatiel is under 6 months old, its coloring is that of a female. Pearl cockatiels have laced feathers that males lose at about 6 months of age. Males will acquire a yellow or white head at that age, too, depending on their color mutation. Cockatiels can live 20 or more years. If you adopt an older bird, you're more likely to know its tameness and vocal abilities. In young chicks, those qualities are unknown, but you have the chance to shape its behavior.

What does the cockatiel eat?

The best answer is a formulated diet with a variety of vegetables for treats. Formulated or manufactured diets are also called *pellets*. They're the equivalent of dog kibble for birds with the vitamins and nutrients parrots require. If you acquire a young bird, a proper diet is very important. The formative weeks are very important to a cockatiel. If she learns to eat a variety of foods, she will continue to try new foods readily. Cockatiels are stubborn about changing their diet. If you acquire a cockatiel who has been eating seeds, switching to a formulated diet is a good idea. Cockatiels can also learn to eat vegetables and treats from you if you're persistent in offering them new foods.

Don't worry about converting a seed-eating cockatiel to a formulated diet in the first month she is with you. A change in environment is already stressful for a cockatiel, so minimize the stress by feeding her a familiar diet. Plan to start your conversion project later.

Is this cockatiel hand tame?

This question is somewhat related to a cockatiel's age. A young cockatiel who is 3 or 4 months old can usually be easily tamed, even if it was raised in an aviary or raised by its cockatiel parents alone. A hand-fed chick is often extremely friendly. A chick that was handled often may need some time to get used to you but will be gentle and will warm to you quickly. Older cockatiels that have been tame usually retain that quality. If an older cockatiel is not hand-tame, you will need to spend more time working with her, and results will vary. Find out what the older cockatiel's strengths are. If she's not a cuddler, perhaps she is a whistler or is willing to be handled with sticks instead of hands. Some cockatiels who don't want to be handled still appreciate a head scratch or can learn to come in and out of their cage and will amuse you with their playfulness.

May I call you if I have questions about my new cockatiel?

It is important for you to have an adviser as you begin cockatiel ownership. Find out whether there's a specific time you should call when you do have questions.

What are the cockatiel's parents like?

You will probably find out about the cockatiel's parents only if you buy a bird from a breeder. Many desirable cockatiel traits seem to be inherited. Are the parents exceptional companion birds? Is dad a good talker? Do they have particularly good size and confirmation? Why did the breeder pair these two birds? Do they have outstanding personalities or are they particularly gorgeous? If you are at all interested in exhibiting your birds or even breeding them, you will want to know what color mutations are in a new cockatiel's background. Exhibitors may want to know whether their new bird comes from a line of show winners. Some cockatiels attain champion and grand champion status on the bird show circuit.

Is this cockatiel banded?

From what organization? What information is on the band? A band is a circular metal ID bracelet that is slipped on a cockatiel as a chick. When the cockatiel is mature, its band does not come off. A band is one of the only ways to permanently identify a bird. Write down your cockatiel's band number and put it in a safe place. The band probably has a year on it and a breeder's code, with a number unique to your chick for that year. It's customary to band birds with a current year's band. Most cockatiels with a band from 2002 will have been hatched in the year 2002. Bands from cockatiel and parrot breeder societies are usually traceable. That is, they keep a record of band numbers and breeder codes so that you can find out who bred the bird you have. Some band companies sell bands to breeders, who make up their own codes and numbers. These bands serve as ID but don't help you find out the origin of a particular cockatiel.

The following organizations issue bands to cockatiel breeders:

- American Cockatiel Society (ACS)
- American Federation of Aviculture (AFA)
- National Cockatiel Society (NCS)
- North American Cockatiel Society (NACS)
- Society of Parrot Breeders and Exhibitors (SPBE)

No federal law requires cockatiels to be banded, and only a few states have regulations on this matter. Your bird may not have a band at all. Your choices for ID include taking some good photos of your bird to have on hand in case it is ever lost or stolen. Write down identifying marks, such as those on the beak or feet, missing toes, or unusual color patterns. It's amazing how alike cockatiels can look, so make your observations carefully and back them up with photographs or video. You may choose to have an *open* band put on your cockatiel. This kind of band is applied on a grown bird and is not seamless. Because of the small opening in the band, it is more dangerous for your bird to wear than a closed band applied to a chick. Parrots can be microchipped, but cockatiels are too small for this method of ID.

Is this a male or female, or a young bird of unknown sex?

Both sexes make good pets, and if you get a chick, the sex may be unknown. Sometimes a breeder sets up pairs where the chicks are of known sex because of their color. That helps you choose a name. Of course, adult cockatiels, except for the pied mutation, have different coloring in the sexes, so you may know the answer to this question by looking at an adult bird.

What color is this cockatiel?

You'll want to know because cockatiels come in many colors. It doesn't matter as far as pet quality is concerned. Any color of cockatiel can be a good companion.

What avian veterinarian do you recommend?

Not every veterinarian treats birds. You will want to know the name of at least one bird vet in your area to schedule a first appointment for your new cockatiel. If you're lucky, you will have a choice of bird vets and can choose one with whom you have a rapport.

What other advice do you have for me?

While you're getting contacts, ask whether you need to know where to get the brand of food you need to feed your cockatiel. Ask about area bird clubs and whether educational classes or seminars are offered in your area. The cockatiel seller, with experience in either raising or keeping cockatiels, is an expert in the services you will need to care for your cockatiel. Take advantage of that expertise.

Adding a Cockatiel to the Family

Your cockatiel will probably take at least two weeks to settle into your home. Expect things to change around your home. Cockatiels have a large presence for little beings! Their cage takes up space. Birds create a mess around their cage, so someone will be cleaning that up, and the rest of your family will be side-stepping the mess. For a while, adding cage clean-up chores to your daily routine will be disrupting. Your household will be a little noisier, too, especially if you already have a noisy household and your cockatiel chimes right in!

You'll want to spend time with your new cockatiel. You can spend some of that time will be simply going about your normal routine with your bird as company. You and your cockatiel will slowly figure out how that routine goes. You may have to establish some rules at breakfast so that your bird knows she can't walk across your cereal bowl and that you know not to offer buttered toast to the feathered member of the family. A cockatiel doesn't need those extra calories from fat, so she'll take plain toast, thank you. Your cockatiel will love to be with you when you brush your teeth or take a shower, and she will delight in mirrors as much as you do. Later in the evening, she'll run up and down the back of your armchair or sofa while you read, study, or watch TV.

Deciding Whether to Get One Cockatiel or Two

I suggest that you get only one cockatiel if you're getting a bird for the first time. A cockatiel is programmed by instinct to join a flock and to bond with its flockmates. To your one cockatiel companion, you become her flock and best friend. If she has a choice of communicating with a cockatiel who speaks its own language or a person of another species, whom do you think the cockatiel will choose to bond to? A single companion cockatiel will bond to you by default. That tameness and closeness will last forever, even if you do decide to get a second cockatiel at a later date.

Eventually, you may decide to get a second cockatiel. A second cockatiel is a companion to your first cockatiel if she is left alone quite a bit during the day or during your extended trips out of town. If the two cockatiels are friends and can share a cage, having two birds isn't really twice as much work as owning one. Two cockatiels can be quieter than one cockatiel, who waits for your attention and demands it with screams and calls. After a year or so of cockatiel ownership, you already know that you can handle bird care — that you are a bird brain! A few more feathers won't likely be a challenge.

You have bonded as a flock with a first cockatiel in your family. Your cockatiel pal may not exactly realize she is a bird! The introduction of a new cockatiel isn't always warmly welcomed by a first cockatiel. She thinks she's a small human. Why should she bother to spend time with a bird?

Other challenges do arise from having two cockatiels, however. The first bird may be jealous or territorial towards a new bird in your family. The feed bills and veterinary bills will double. Incentive for breeding behavior will be more likely if you have a male and female cockatiel together, doing what comes naturally. Cockatiels are a species who are always ready to breed and who aren't programmed to limit breeding to a certain season of the year.

If you enjoy having one cockatiel, you may be tempted to get more. Try to remember to keep the bird count at your house down to a number with whom you can interact regularly and care for appropriately.

Naming Your New Cockatiels

A cockatiel can learn its name. Whatever name you decide on for your little friend, she will live with it for 20 years or more, so take your time. Of course, the decision about what to name your cockatiel is very personal and entirely up to you. While you're tossing names around and trying them on your new friend, here are some ideas of sources of both common and uncommon cockatiel names! One of the big challenges with naming chicks is that you don't know the sex of the youngest cockatiels until they attain their adult coloring at the age of about 6 months. You may need a little help coming up with a unisex name.

Look up names in a baby book

Names have meanings, and sometimes flipping through a baby book helps you choose a name that matches the personality of your new cockatiel. You can match the name to your heritage or the cockatiel's sex, or you can choose a name that has special meaning. You can find baby books at book-stores and libraries, and you also can check out lists of potential names on Web sites. Search for "pet bird names" or "pet names" for ideas. Some of the sites available include the following:

✔ http://www.cybercomm.net/~goldie/names.html

✔ http://pets.indya.com/pets/petnames/birds/main.html

✔ http://homearts.com/depts/pastime/petnam16.htm

✔ http://IVAnimalRescue.tripod.com/names.html

Consider the color of your cockatiel

Your cockatiel has a color that may remind you of some object or person. Cinnamon cockatiels may just need to be called Cinnamon, Cocoa, or Brownie. Lutino and albino cockatiels look like Snowy, Popcorn, Lemontop, or Meringue. Gray and whiteface cockatiels may respond to Argent, Baldy, Silver, Charcoal, or Norm (for normal gray!?). The patterning on a boldly colored cockatiel may inspire Lacey as a name for a pearl. There's always the name Pearl, too, or even Minnie Pearl. Jester, Harlequin, Patches, and Bozo come to mind for those wild pieds. Use your imagination, and I'm sure you can think of a few appropriate color-related potential names for your cockatiel.

Add international flair

If you have studied a foreign language, admire another culture, have traveled abroad, or are close to your own foreign roots, you can probably come up with some great cockatiel names. How about Francois or Nicole, Anastasia or Nicholas, Pablo or Miguel? You can take your inspiration from geography, cuisine, or cultural heroes. Maybe you don't want to name your cockatiel Omelet because he's escaped that phase of being an egg, but you could try Mignon or Ratatouille, Ragout or Ravioli. There's always Paris, Munich, Florence, Roma, de Gaulle, Tutu, or Gandhi.

Consider Australian geography

Cockatiels are natives of Australia, so about every third cockatiel is named Sydney. You could continue that trend, or look up a few of the cities in Australia that have interesting names. Does Brisbane, Perth, Ayers (for Ayers Rock), Canberra, Adelaide, or Melbourne strike your fancy? Or even Victoria or Darwin or Hobart. Go wild!

Think of famous people

You can also name a cockatiel after a famous person, such as a political figure, a musician, an actor, or a character in a sitcom. You could name your cockatiel after a famous movie star, a painter, a ballet dancer, or a race horse. Try on first names, last names, and nicknames. Have fun! Some people are famous only to you. It is a special honor to name your pet after your favorite person. Remember that you and your bird will live with this name for up to 20 years. Don't be tempted to get revenge this way.

Let your cockatiel name itself

I think Squirt and Squawk or Chippy and Chirp show how a cockatiel can name herself. A few cockatiels out there are named Baby their whole life. Pretty Boy may be a talker, as may Loquacious. The occasional Lucky finds a loving home or escapes an accident. Use your cockatiel's demeanor, vocalizations, and attitude to help you decide on a name.

Refer to the family crest

Cockatiels aren't the only ones with crests in the family. Look up the name of a great grandparent or name your bird after your sister or the family dog. You can also consider locations that mean family to you. What was the name of the little town where you went every summer?

Part II

Cockatiel Care

The 5th Wave By Rich Tennant

"The birds diet is regulated pretty carefully, except when Doug falls asleep after dinner with his mouth open."

In this part . . .

Caring for your cockatiel involves many different
tasks, all of which I cover in this part. I describe the
items your cockatiel needs — from a cage to food — and I
give you the basics on how to keep your cockatiel happy,
healthy, and well groomed.

Chapter 3

Home Tweet Home

*O*nce you've chosen a cockatiel for your very own, it's time to bring him into your home. Expect some changes! Despite their small size, cockatiels can take up a bit of room and a bit of your time once they've moved into your life. You'll want to make a wise choice about the location of the cockatiel's enclosure. You also want to make the cockatiel as comfortable as possible in his new home. You want to be able to keep a cockatiel's environment clean and safe. You ought to have access to your little feathered friend to give him the socialization time he needs now that you're his flock. Especially if your new cockatiel is a chick, he will look to you for companionship and for guidance.

Those first couple weeks will be the most challenging for both of you. They'll also be fun. You'll be getting to know each other and establishing routines for the coming years. The transition will be easier if the person who sold your cockatiel to you has properly educated you about cockatiel ownership. If you know how to handle your bird and what food he has been eating, you can treat him to some familiar things amidst all the new stimuli of your household. Having a new pet in the household upsets the balance somewhat. You'll need to find out what time works for you to care for and play with your new cockatiel. Relationships may need to be established between your new bird and the other people as well as the other pets in a household. If you have a companion bird already, this adjustment will be delayed while you quarantine your new cockatiel.

Think about where you place your cockatiel's cage and what kind of cage you can provide him. No cage is too big for a pet that's built to soar through the skies on a daily basis. That means you could convert an alcove, set up an indoor aviary, or make a large play area outside of a cage for your cockatiel to inhabit. Your cockatiel may be more mobile than you think. He'll enjoy being with you during your daily activities. Set up play areas or perches in different areas of your home to give him some stimulation and opportunity to travel. He's already taking up more of your house than the corner of the living room you set aside for him, isn't he?

Making Your Cockatiel Feel at Home

Your new cockatiel may immediately make himself at home in your house. It's more likely, however, that your little friend will be stressed by the changes in his life and lifestyle. He has left other cockatiels and a nurturing hand feeder or parents. He's had a certain schedule for the first few weeks of his life, which is all changing. The environment and the people in his life are different now. Stress will show up in many ways. You may have a depressed cockatiel for a while. He may be sleepy or listless. His digestive system, which has been changing rapidly as he changed from being fed to eating on his own, may be upset or may still be undergoing that change. Chicks in the nest have large, whitish droppings. Weaned chicks eventually have adult droppings consisting of a watery component, white solids, and a colored tubular component. He may scream, calling for what he considers the rest of his flock, his clutchmates, or the people in his former life. All of these behavioral changes can also signal illness. If your new cockatiel is harboring an infection or an illness, his stress could trigger more symptoms. That's why a well-bird checkup with an avian veterinarian soon after you get your cockatiel helps you sort out the signals you're getting.

One way stress may show up in a young chick is in watery droppings. If this occurs for a day or two when you first get your cockatiel, it is probably not cause for alarm. If the condition continues, however, do seek veterinary advice.

One lesson that cockatiels have for us is to "be" in the present. Though a change in lifestyle is stressful, your cockatiel will not spend much time regretting the past. His adjustment time will be fast as he throws himself into life with you.

Why quarantining is good

If the cockatiel is not your first bird in your house, you should quarantine the new arrival for at least a month. This procedure safeguards the health of the well-loved and well-established cockatiel already living in your home. We've been learning a lot about bird diseases over the last two decades, but we probably have more to learn. Birds make it a challenge to know when they are sick. They don't often show signs of illness because they're prey animals who would quickly be dinner if they didn't keep up with their flock. Quarantine of a new arrival is the safest procedure to follow.

Quarantine of a companion cockatiel means that you keep the bird separate from your other birds. Ideally, you should keep a quarantined cockatiel in a separate building. In reality, most people quarantine new birds in a separate room of their home. This quarantine period gives you time to examine the new bird for symptoms of illness and to take it to the veterinarian to confirm his health. Treat this bird as though he does have an illness that would be contagious to your other bird or birds. Clean his cage last. Wash your hands after handling him. Don't wear shoes from his room to the room where your other pet bird is because they could track dust and airborne illness. If you have a smock or separate top to wear in the quarantine area, that's even better.

When the quarantine is over, and if you detected no sign of illness, you can take your new cockatiel and his cage to join the family, including your other birds! Give your cockatiel some time to adjust to his new surroundings if he needs it. Let him stay in his cage and look around unless he's one of the gregarious cockatiels who doesn't need much adjustment time. He just needs to be out exploring.

Why change is bad

You can make a new cockatiel's adjustment to your household much easier if you don't change all his familiar routines and possessions. For example, don't worry about changing the diet of your new cockatiel right away. He's facing enough changes for now; you can work on the diet later. Did your cockatiel have a favorite toy, perch, or swing? Buying a similar one will make this new place seem familiar. If the cockatiel was offered a bowl for bathing or had learned to be showered regularly, you can do this for him as well. Offer the cockatiel his favorite food and treats. If your cockatiel is a "used pet," find out the words he knows — both the words he can say and the ones that he reacts to.

Feeding Your Young Bird

If you're bringing a cockatiel into your home who is under 4 months old, his beak is probably not as hard as an adult's beak. He will appreciate having an abundance of soft foods during this stage. Cockatiels at this age also need a lot more calcium, protein, and fat than older birds. You can feed them a *breeder pellet* during this time or supplement their formulated diet while they're growing. I hope the store or breeder where you got your cockatiel explained your chick's dietary needs and let you know what the bird was accustomed to eating. You also may find it helpful to know how the bird was fed when it was weaning — was food placed on the floor of the cage (normal for weaning chicks) or in bowls? If you don't know how your cockatiel was being fed, try several techniques and help your chick along by showing him where the food is and what to do with that food! Go ahead and pretend to eat some pellets yourself within view of your cockatiel. Yum!

Here are appropriate soft foods for cockatiels under 4 months old:

- Air-popped popcorn
- Broccoli slaw
- Cornbread
- Grated vegetables
- Millet spray
- Parsley
- Scrambled egg
- Thawed frozen corn
- Thawed frozen peas
- Toasted oat cereal
- Warm oatmeal
- Whole wheat bread

Chapter 4 covers diet in even more detail. A cockatiel's diet doesn't stay as elaborate as it is for a young chick. After a spurt of growth as a chick, a companion cockatiel can eat a maintenance diet to maintain his energy and health. Two to three months old is a *teething stage* for young cockatiels. Because cockatiels don't have teeth, this behavior is rather remarkable. At this stage, a cockatiel is learning how and what to eat, and he is hungry! Between the time a cockatiel is 4 weeks old (and being hand-fed every meal) and the time it is weaned, flying, and on its own, he has actually lost some weight. Your cockatiel will be ready to make up for this loss by chewing on everything in sight. Of course, this is a good time to offer a variety of food. By doing so, you train your cockatiel to become an adult who accepts new foods and diet changes. It is also a good time to hold a toy or treat when you hold your cockatiel. Your cockatiel will test your fingers and clothes along with the rest of its environment. Teach him to chew on acceptable toys and to eat treats, not your sweater. This time in your bird's life is a golden opportunity to encourage good behavior.

While your cockatiel is teething, he will also be testing just what his beak can do to you. You probably already have a general idea, which is why you don't want too much testing going on. Let your cockatiel know when he bites down instead of just mouthing you. He should understand the tone in your voice and limit himself to a gentler touch. If he nibbles at you too often, you can gently shake him, with no other words or explanation. He'll be knocked slightly off balance by a force that feels like an earthquake to him. He'll get the hint if you're consistent. With a cockatiel chick in the house, you're taking on the task of teaching your bird the skills he never learned from his parents.

Making a Place for Your Bird at Home

Your cockatiel will need a space he can call his own in your house. He is a sociable little bird who wants to be a part of the flock at your house. He'll need to be in an area of the house where there's lots of foot traffic, where he can greet and interact with the most people, and where he can see what's happening in the household. That way you can be in voice communication with her, even when he's not out socializing. He'll also feel included in conversations, movie watching, and other family activities. Undoubtedly he'll join in, whether he's invited or not. A cage should be considered your cockatiel's safe spot in the house — his retreat and dining room and bedroom. When you're home, though, allow your bird to be out and about. He'll enjoy doing even the most mundane activities with you, which really makes him a part of your flock. Just because your bird has a cage doesn't mean he always needs to be confined to it.

Finding the ideal location

You want your cockatiel to be in a safe location. One room where you shouldn't put your cockatiel is in the kitchen, where the dangers range from fumes and smoke to open pots of boiling water.

Another unsafe location for a caged cockatiel is by a window exposed to full sunlight. Your cockatiel may like to sunbathe and look out at its wild cousins, but he needs to be able to cool off from the effect of the sun's burning rays. Windows just inside sun-screening awnings or windows overlooking a porch are better choices than windows in full sun.

If you had your heart set on having your cockatiel in a certain room but you can see now that it isn't a good idea, never fear. You can always set up a perch or play gym in that room so that the cockatiel can spend some time there with you, even if it isn't the location of his sleeping cage.

Lethal cookware

The most dangerous item in a kitchen is a non-stick pan. If you accidentally leave a pan on the stove or let it boil dry and it overheats, it emits a gas that is deadly to birds — within minutes. The safest thing for bird owners is to use other types of cookware. If your do accidentally over-heat a nonstick pan, ventilate the area quickly to try to dissipate the gas before it does any harm.

Dealing with the mess

Without a doubt, your cockatiel will create a mess. I can guarantee it. But you can take some steps to reduce the mess. For example, consider the kind of flooring you have around your cockatiel's cage and how you can protect it. Linoleum is easy to clean and a wise choice. If you have carpeting, you can protect it with a chair mat designed to allow office chairs to roll on carpeting, or with a remnant of indoor-outdoor carpet. If you're a renter and want to keep your flooring looking good for the next tenant, consider putting down a rug or carpet remnant in a small area. You can roll that up and move it with you or toss it, depending on how well used it becomes.

High-gloss enamel on walls washes well. If your walls have a matte finish or you're protecting wallpaper, you may want to hang heavy plastic or shower curtains behind the bird cages. Both are washable when they get dirty and disposable when they become worn.

Be careful about the kind of furniture and household equipment around the your cockatiel's cage. Cockatiels are one species of bird whose down feathers disintegrate into a fine powder. This powder settles on electronic items and can cause problems. I don't advise setting up your cockatiel's home near a computer or stereo equipment for that reason. Or if you do, invest in an air filter and use it faithfully. The powder from the feathers also makes book-cases difficult to keep clean.

Considering the noise

Another factor to consider when setting up your cockatiel's home is noise. Your bird will try to keep up with the level of noise in the room where he is located. If your hard-of-hearing uncle or resident teen has the TV blasting in the living room, think about what the din will be with the addition of cock-atiel squawks. Males especially have loud voices and chime right in to the music or TV with their screams and whistles. A female can scream, and she can learn to ring a bell loudly if one is available.

Full spectrum lighting

Sunbathing is beneficial for cockatiels. It gives them a chance to absorb natural vitamin D3 from sunlight and "talk" to wild birds while their cage airs out. Be sure to offer a bird shade as well as light and cooling sprays of water while he's outside. Another advantage of sunbathing is that you can see the "true colors" of your magnificent bird because indoor lighting usually casts an artificial light. However, cockatiel owners may not always be able to give their bird outside time. In that case, you can offer some of the benefits of sunlight by having a full-spectrum light near your cockatiel's cage. Full-spectrum lighting, which is available through fluorescent tubes, mimics the spectrum of sunlight. Unlike plant or reptile lighting, full-spectrum lighting isn't meant to produce heat. Its benefits haven't ever been fully explained, but it may do good and doesn't do harm to your cockatiel. Be sure to read the instructions carefully when you buy a full-spectrum light. Often, a full-spectrum light is good only for a year, though the light will continue to burn longer than that. Mark bulb replacement on your calendar so you remember when it's time to buy a new light.

Warning: If your cockatiel starts to pant and hold his wings away from his body, he is overheating. Spray him with a misty shower of water and get him in out of the sun. A cockatiel spending time outside should also have a shady retreat.

Watching other pets

If you keep any predatory animals — including dogs, cats, ferrets, or hawks — as household pets, think about the safety of your cockatiel around those animals. A cockatiel is low on the food chain and may look like a nice meal to animals who by instinct prey on small birds. Keep your cockatiel's safety in mind when setting up a cage and make sure that you can supervise interaction between your cockatiel and your other pets. For example, locate your cockatiel in a room with doors that can be shut so that it is off limits to the family cats. You may need to let a cockatiel live in a bedroom and come out only when your cat or dog is either confined or supervised by you. Training and gates may solve your problem with regard to the co-mingling of species in your home.

Housing Options

Research has shown that your cockatiel will be happiest in the kind of enclosure he is used to. If you're getting a used cockatiel, hopefully his home tweet home comes along with the bird. You can upgrade after your new cockatiel becomes a member of the family. Your young chick is adaptable. He'll be most comfortable in the size cage he grew up in, but he'll learn to like any cage that is of adequate size. The sky's the limit. But come to think of it, probably the sky and the open are the last place you want to see your cockatiel.

You have some options in cockatiel enclosures. You can build an outside aviary or an inside aviary. Preconstructed versions of both are available. You can build a cockatiel habitat from an alcove or a room in your house. You can buy large, powder-coated, heavy parrot cages for your cockatiel. You can buy cockatiel enclosures that are as handsome as furniture or others that are utilitarian wire. You need to consider several factors when looking for that special abode for your cockatiel.

Cost

There is a practical side to cockatiel housing. Your price range may limit your choices to some extent. But try to think big even with a small budget. A cockatiel enclosure may cost from $55 for an adequate cage that on sale, about $120 for a roomy cage for one to two cockatiels, or over $300 for an aviary.

Comfort

Your cockatiel will go to the top of any cage you get. For that reason, long cages are preferable to tall cages. To your cockatiel, a cage is only as big as its length and width. Your cockatiel will spend most of his time at the top of any cage you provide, so height isn't important. Get a cage that is a minimum of two feet long. Your cockatiel deserves some room for play and exercise.

Bar spacing

Cockatiels know a lot about Murphy's Law and tempt it. Instead of "whatever can go wrong will go wrong," they chime in with "whatever trouble I can get into, I will." And the wrong type of cage can lead to trouble. Cockatiels are curious about everything, and they know the grass is greener, the feed is fresher, and there's more fun on the other side of the bars! Bar spacing on your cage should be close enough together that your cockatiel can't get his head through the bars. Bars that are ½ inch apart are great, but bars that are ¾ inch apart will probably be fine.

While I'm talking about cage bars, check that they're made of something safe. Aviary wire is utilitarian, but if a bird chews on the wire, he could very well get zinc poisoning. You can do your best to prevent this by washing new cages or new wire with a vinegar solution before it is used. Cast-iron cages may be welded with lead solder, which is not safe for a cockatiel. They may nibble or chew on the lead and get heavy metal poisoning. You can use a lead test kit (made for the safety of children) to find out if there is a problem with a cage. Most cast iron and large cages have a heavy-duty baked-on finish called powder coating. Occasionally this powder coating has been found to contain zinc. That's only a problem if your cockatiel chews off flakes of the baked-on finish. There aren't home tests for zinc, you would need to contact the manufacturer about the paint used (preferably before buying a cage) or send samples to a lab to ensure the safety of your cockatiel. Zinc poisoning is also a heavy metal poisoning. Either lead or zinc poisoning can be treated by your veterinarian, but its best not to expose your cockatiel to risk. Many cockatiel cages are made safely of cage wire, which becomes unsafe only if it gets rusty and the cockatiel eats flakes of metal. A rusty used cage isn't a good choice of home for your new cockatiel.

Cleaning

Keeping an accommodation clean probably isn't the first thing you think about when choosing a cage. If your new cage is a bear to clean, however, you'll be reminded on a daily basis. Rectangular cages clean much easier than round cages, simply because you can more easily fold newspaper into the bottom of them. A cage with a grate helps separate a cockatiel from droppings and used food, though you'll want to wipe off the grate often. A deep tray under the grate is easier to clean than a skimpy tray. You may or may not want the shields that extend out from some bird cages. Yes, they keep droppings from soiling the floor. But guess where the droppings land? On the shield. Then you need to wipe the shield clean frequently. Another feature that makes cleaning easier is a nice big door, so that you can reach in easily. Make sure that you can reach every corner of an enclosure. Some larger enclosures literally don't allow for cleaning every corner without a high-powered hose.

Expansion

Are you absolutely sure that you're a one-cockatiel family? If so, then get a cage for one cockatiel. If you get a roomy cage that can house two or three cockatiels, you may be tempting fate. It won't be too big for your first cockatiel, but just in case, you'd be ready for the next member of the family.

Very few bird owners have just one bird. I don't know what it is about birds, especially cockatiels, but they take over our hearts, and usually several end up sharing our homes with us.

Access to bowls in a cage

If a relative or bird sitter is afraid of birds (what, your little sweetie?) or doesn't know how to handle them, they'll really appreciate the fact that your cockatiel's food and water bowls are accessible from outside the cage. You really need three or four bowls to serve your cockatiel feed, water, vegetables, and treats. For some reason, most cockatiel cages come equipped two bowls, but you can buy additional treat cups to place inside the cage. It is usually a good idea to have more bowls than are provided with most cages.

Open sesame

Look for a cage with a big front door. Cockatiels are fairly large for small birds, so they don't exit easily out of a smaller door meant for a parakeet. They also learn quickly to latch onto the entryway of a small doorway. Then you assume your cockatiel is coming out on your finger, but he will remain behind where he's grabbed onto the cage. When you need to reach into the cage, you too will appreciate the room you have to maneuver through a large cage door. Some doors convert to perches, as do the tops of some cages. With those features, you don't need to buy extra cage-top perch equipment.

Other openings in a cage are useful. If there's any chance you'd ever breed cockatiels, a pre-made opening high in the cage, where a nest box can be attached, is very useful. The alternative is cutting a hole in a perfectly good cage, a step that seems wasteful and isn't usually pretty.

Just for show

Safety should be your first concern when buying a cage. Curlicues and ornaments on a cage with no purpose can be hazards. A cockatiel could get his band or a wing wedged in a tight place. Similarly, if a round cage has wire bars that narrow as they come together on top that poses a danger. Look at a cage as though you're the embodiment of curiosity, and try to figure out what trouble you could get into if you lived in it.

The Bottom of the Cage

Placing newspapers on the bottom of a bird cage is a long-established practice among bird owners and still a great option (see Figure 3-1). Newspaper is readily available, and if printed with soy ink, it won't hurt your bird, who will inevitably chew on it. Newspaper allows you to check your cockatiel's droppings daily. Bird droppings are an important indicator of health, and at first it shows whether your cockatiel is eating.

Figure 3-1:
Newspaper
is still the
best cover
for the
bottom of
the cage.

You can also use other types of paper on the bottom of bird cages, provided that they're safe for your cockatiel. You can get unprinted newspaper from your city's newspaper office. Ask for the end rolls, which are available for free or for a small fee. They make great mural paper for kids, too. Butcher paper, kraft paper, and computer paper also work for your bird cage, depending on what you have available to you. They all can be cut and folded to fit the bottom of a cage. Change the cage paper daily. Daily means every day. No slacking. Your cockatiel's health depends on it.

If you want to make changing bird papers easier, go ahead and stack papers up in the tray that holds paper for your cage. Then roll up the top layer of soiled paper, and you're ready for another day.

I discourage any kind of bedding that allows you to be lazy about cleaning your cockatiel's cage. Don't use pine shavings, walnut shells, or corn cob bedding. Don't tear up newspaper or pour in clean sand. You probably won't be inclined to change these substrates very often, allowing mold and bacteria to grow. These types of bedding materials also don't allow you to check the color and consistency of your cockatiel's droppings.

Cleaning Up

You'll find that you're always using your vacuum around a cockatiel cage. You may want to dedicate a handheld vacuum to the chore of whisking up feed, debris, and dust around a cockatiel cage. A broom works well, too. For droppings, soap and water do the job. Cockatiel droppings are odorless and water soluble. They aren't a big mess, but things look neater when you take care of them on a regular basis by scrubbing the walls, vacuuming the floor, and wiping off the cage. Keep tissues on hand for the small jobs. You may want to wear a bird shirt when your cockatiel is out and about on your shoulders. Or wear a towel over your clothing.

Disinfect the cockatiel's cage at least monthly. Take out all the bowls and toys. Wipe the cage off or immerse it in a solution of nine parts water and one part bleach. Soak bowls in the solution for ten to fifteen minutes. Rinse everything in clear water and allow them to dry. Bleach solution doesn't keep well — it is broken down by air and light — so make only what you can use and discard the rest. You can use other disinfectants, but few are as friendly to the environment as bleach.

Your cockatiel will probably live in its new home for years to come. Set up an area for your cockatiel's cage that allows you to keep it clean and lets the bird visit with family members. With wise choices in location and cage, you'll both be happy.

Use a night light

Cockatiels, more than other species of companion birds, are prone to night frights. Occasionally in the dark, they start to thrash about their cage wildly, flying into the bars and potentially hurting themselves. Cockatiels don't see well in the dark, and in their panic they aren't paying much attention. A night light near a cockatiel cage is a measure of prevention against night frights. A light also gives your cockatiel a chance to find his perch after a fright. Call it the night fright night light.

Chapter 4

Eating Like a Bird

. . . .

. . . .

Despite a common belief, if we ate like a bird, we wouldn't be scrawny! Birds have high metabolisms, and for their body weight, they eat quite a bit of food. Cockatiels munch all of their fare without teeth. (At least you're spared dental bills for your birds.) They use their remarkable beaks and a rubber eraser-like tongue to crunch hard treats and take seeds out of their hulls. Cockatiels are a forgiving species of bird, in that they are adapted to harsh desert conditions. They've become popular pets over the last 150 years because they survive even if offered a minimum of care and a marginal diet. You want your cockatiel to do more than survive, however. You want him to thrive, enjoy his life and your company, and live a long, happy life. A healthy diet can help your cockatiel do all these things.

The basic diet of our companion cockatiels for the past 150 years has been seed and water. Veterinarians eventually noticed, however, that many birds in their practice had diseases related to malnutrition, and they sometimes died from it. As a result, long-term studies were done that concluded that a diet richer in nutrients and more complete in amino acids is better for cockatiels than seeds. Now we can offer formulated diets akin to kibble for dogs to our companion birds as a basic staple of their diet. Kibble alone is not enough for our intelligent pets. Keep your kitchen knives and the food processor handy. A diet supplemented with fresh vegetables offers the variety and stimulation on which our intelligent cockatiels thrive.

There's also something heartwarming about being able to offer a cockatiel something daily that he delights in. You'll develop a closer bond with your cockatiel as you stay creative in your daily treat offering and because you're taking the time to prepare it. Your cockatiel will become closer to you because you take the time to interact with him daily. And that interaction involves food — a definite favorite of cockatiels. This ritual, which you can look forward to for years to come, cements the cockatiel-human relationship.

A Drop or Two to Drink

Cockatiels don't drink a lot of water because they've adapted to living in the desert. They do require some water to live, however. That water should be clean, healthy, and free of debris. A good test is to look in your cockatiel's water container. Would you be willing to drink that water? If not, change it.

Your cockatiel's water should be so clean that you would be willing to drink it. You may need to change the water in your bird's cage several times a day. At least once is mandatory!

Water flows out of our taps, comes in bottles, gets delivered to our door, and flows in the wild. Water comes from the garden hose, the well, and the kitchen sink! There's everyday water and emergency water. Whatever concerns you have about the safety of your water supply applies as much or more so to your cockatiel. He has a smaller body and a higher susceptibility to toxins. Your cockatiel can't get his own water either, so seeing that he has clean water is your responsibility.

If you use an outside hose to fill your cockatiel's water bowls or to clean his cage, let the water run at least two minutes before filling a bowl. Bacteria that is harmful to your bird can grow in the water hose.

With a bird's tendency to develop bacterial infections, providing clean, filtered water is one of your best ways of preventing them. You can install a filter on your faucet or use a pitcher that filters your tap water. Bottled water is a second-best choice. Be aware that it can develop bacteria if it sits around for a while, however. If you have a dispenser in your home, keep it clean. If you buy bottled water, be sure to rotate the bottles so that you have some on hand and are using up the oldest stock. You may handle well water . . . er . . . well, but birds are more easily affected by bacteria and parasites than humans. Certainly filter or treat well water before providing it to your birds.

You can buy various powders and substances to mix with your cockatiel's water. Offering your cockatiel anything but clean, pure water, however, isn't a good idea. Because cockatiels don't drink much, they won't get an appropriate dose of vitamins or medication if offered in water. If they don't like the taste, they may even refuse to drink. Some vitamins are water soluble and quickly lose their nutrient value. If you feed a formulated diet, supplemental vitamins aren't necessary at all. If a cockatiel bathes in water containing a substance, chances are good that he will get sticky feathers and lose the ability to regulate its body temperature. The message is simple: Serve just plain, pure water.

Choosing a Water Container: Belly on Up to the H₂0 Bar

An array of containers is available for serving water to your cockatiel. You can choose bowls, tubes, cups, bottles, or even automatic water sources. Some water receptacles are designed for the inside of the cage, and others are made for the outside. To some extent, your choice will be determined by the style of your cage or other enclosure. Look for a bowl that your bird can reach easily and that you can clean easily. You may use the bowl provided in your cage, or you can buy one that attaches to the cage bar.

Some large, flat containers are not suitable for your bird's drinking water because they become bathtubs — and how would you like to drink bath water? Your cockatiel won't appreciate it either, although he will enjoy the occasional bath. Bowls with hoods aren't acceptable for cockatiels either because they're shy about putting their head into the enclosed space.

The advantage of a bowl is that it is a readily available accessory for your cage, it is easy to clean out, and you can see when it's dirty. Bowls, however, are a problem for people whose cockatiels are "dunkers" who confuse their pellets and water with coffee and donuts. (Maybe they're learning more from you than you think.) For the dunkers, try another system of providing water. Tubes and bottles are available that hang on the outside of a cage and have a small bowl that goes to the inside of a cage, allowing a cockatiel to drink from it. Glass tubes need to scrubbed regularly so that slime doesn't build up in them. Likewise, water bottles need to be scrubbed out, with special attention to the tubes where crud may build up.

Glass tubes are relatively fragile. Keep an extra one on hand and handle with care!

Water bottles for your cockatiel look like the water bottles you might get for a rodent pet. They have a large water receptacle that hangs outside of a cage, and a tube that goes into a cage with a ball in it that prevents water from spilling or, when moved, allows water to flow. This bottle is a little trickier for a cockatiel to drink from. Of course cockatiels are clever enough to figure it out quickly! At first, place a water bottle tube near the water bowl. Your cockatiel probably won't be able to resist inspecting this new toy. When you're certain he knows how to get water from a tube, you can remove the water dish from his cage.

Placement of bowls and drinkers

It usually works best to place bowls at mid-level in a cage. Certainly, don't place perches over the water, or that water isn't going to stay clean for long. You may find that water bowls located up high in a cage are attractive night perches for your cockatiels. As a result, the bowls are very dirty in the morning! Experiment with placement until you know you can keep your cockatiel's water clean.

Alternative water containers are glass tubes that hang on the outside of a cage and allow a cockatiel access to water at a plastic base which fits into the cage. Water bottles that dispense water through a stainless steel tube-and-ball mechanism protrude into a cage from outside as well. These water containers don't make good perches, so you don't have to worry about having them fill with droppings. You can make your needs number one and put a water tube or bottle in a location that makes it easy for you to fill. You'll also want to make sure you can check the water level easily. Inventive or bored cockatiels may figure out how to drain a water bottle fast by playing with the water tube.

Placement of the water receptacle is an important consideration. "Poop soup" is not an ideal beverage, so don't place the water bowl where droppings are likely to fall into the water. You also need to try to keep food out of the water. If you separate the food and water containers by placing them on the opposite sides of a cage, you give your bird an additional benefit — some incentive to get regular exercise.

Clean the water receptacles with soap and water at least daily. Disinfect them about once per week by soaking them in a 10-percent bleach solution for about 15 minutes. The materials that stand up best to this treatment are ceramics, glass, and stainless steel. Aluminum and zinc-coated bowls react with bleach, while plastic may become slimy faster than the harder, nonporous materials.

Formulated Diets

Formulated diets for birds offer the same convenience as prepared kibble that you feed your dog or cat and also provide nutrition in every bite. Birds are smaller animals than your dog or cat, however, so a kibble for a cockatiel is a small crumble, pellet, or bead of food.

Formulated diets are prepared foods for your cockatiel. They are formed from a mash of grain mixed with vitamins and minerals that is formed into pellets or shapes, and they are designed to meet your cockatiel's nutritional needs. Bird kibbles are usually called pellets, formulated diets, or manufactured diets. Many are referred to by the brand name or manufacturer's name. This food should be the basis of your cockatiel's diet, so it should be available in a dish in his cage at all times. The rest of the diet for your companion cockatiel should consist of low-calorie vegetable and grain treats.

Of course, seed diets have long been considered a diet for our cockatiel companions. We know now that they don't provide a cockatiel with everything he needs in his diet, so a formulated diet should be your first choice of diet for your cockatiel. In fact, it's a good idea to choose a cockatiel from someone who is feeding a formulated diet to his birds. Cockatiels are creatures of habit and stubborn about huge lifestyle changes, such as changes in what they eat. They become "seed junkies" — addicted to seed — and refuse to willingly eat a formulated diet or to add vegetables to their diet. You're the one who must decide that a formulated diet is best for your bird — your bird is not likely to suddenly decide for himself that he likes a formulated diet. We cover changing diet later in this chapter. This is the first step in that process: making the decision to feed your cockatiel a formulated diet.

All formulated diets are not equal. Most offer your bird a good base diet, but some add colors or flavors that are meant to appeal more to a human buying bird food, than to a bird's need for a healthful diet. Avoid the diets with added color and sugar.

Generally, you'll be choosing a fairly small size formulated diet for your cockatiel. It may be formed into geometric shapes, crumbled, round balls, or pellets. Your cockatiel will eat a formulated diet as though it is a seed, leaving a powdery residue in his cup. Wild birds may enjoy the leftovers. Your cockatiel will also eat this powder if it's left as the only food, but he prefers to have fresh new food to crunch up.

When purchasing a formulated diet, buy sealed packages rather than loose food from bulk bins. Many avian diseases are carried by dust or are passed in the air. Food that has not been exposed to air is safest for your bird, especially if that air has had other birds in it! If you buy more formulated diet than you can use in a short time, you may freeze the extra.

All-natural formulated bird diets

Some buyers object to the addition of chemical preservatives to formulated diets and prefer the natural recipes. That is in part a personal choice. Birds are susceptible to molds and bacteria, so if you purchase a food without preservatives, ensure that it is fresh and that you store it in a cool, dry place. Bird food manufacturers use only preservatives that have been proven to be safe to people and animals. For example, unsubstantiated negative stories about the preservative ethoxyquin have circulated that aren't backed up by science. Because your bird's food must be free of molds and bacteria, some kind of preservative is advantageous in his food. Enough birds have been eating formulated diets for enough years to prove that such diets improve nutrition more than seed diets do. A formulated diet is a good choice.

We don't know a lot about allergies in birds yet. Formulated diets are made from different grains. Do these ingredients affect cockatiels? We don't know, but it's one factor you and your avian veterinarian should consider if your cockatiel has unusual behavior or health problems.

Changing Your Bird's Diet

Even though you know that a formulated diet is best for your cockatiel, you may have a difficult time convincing your bird of this! Cockatiels get stuck in a food rut easily, eating only a few items and not making the best choices. You need to take the initiative to convert a cockatiel to a formulated diet. Some of the same techniques that can change a bird's diet from seeds to kibble can be used to change a bird's diet so that he includes more healthy and fun vegetable snacks in his diet.

Converting your bird's diet from seeds to pellets sounds easy. You may think that you can just put some formulated diet in the cage with a cockatiel and he'll start eating it. You have about as much chance of success with that approach as you would if you served quiche to a Little League team. Seeds are the cockatiel's version of ice cream — they're full of good-tasting fat. Think of this analogy if you're having trouble understanding why your cockatiel may turn up his beak at the pellets: If you were offered a choice between ice cream and spinach salad, what would you choose?

Another problem with changing your bird's diet is that a cockatiel probably doesn't even realize that a formulated diet is really food when he first sees it in a dish. He's used to the familiar shapes and colors of seeds and may not recognize food without hulls.

Your cockatiel should be healthy and happy before you attempt to change his diet. If he is new in your household or is battling an infection or illness, wait a while. Changing diet is a stress to your cockatiel, though one that is good for his health in the long run.

Some people try to change their bird's diet by emptying out a cockatiel's seed dish and filling it with formulated diet. That technique may work for some cockatiels. But, of course, this is *your* bird I'm talking about, so if this method doesn't work, you don't want to starve your friend.

The best way to convert a cockatiel to a formulated diet is to offer him the formulated diet in his normal seed cup during the day. Start the day out that way and leave that food in the cup till evening. Offer him a couple teaspoons of his normal seed in the evening. Take the seed away overnight and start out the next morning with only formulated diet again. Your cockatiel has a chance to find the formulated diet during the day, and peck at it. He may try to avoid it at first, not recognizing the kibble as food. As your cockatiel becomes curious about what's in his feed dish, he will investigate it. Eventually, he'll crumble it up and eat it. This conversion method takes a couple weeks to cause a change in diet. You need to be consistent and persistent. Your bird may vocalize or pace when you come home in the evening, anticipating its seed for dinner.

You can do many things to help your cockatiel recognize that these little rocks in his cage are really edible. Remember that cockatiels instinctively want to be part of a flock. At your house, that flock consists of you and your family. You can use this to your advantage by pretending to eat and enjoy formulated diet within view of your cockatiel. Your cockatiel probably eats dinner when you do, so that's a good time to pretend to join your cockatiel in eating formulated diet. Make your enjoyment obvious and exaggerated — *mmmm, this is good!*

If you're working on converting a bird who is not your only cockatiel, then another bird in the same cage can be its flock mate and ably demonstrate that eating a formulated diet is the way to go. Older cockatiels can teach younger ones, or young teenage cockatiels (4 to 18 months old) with their voracious appetites can teach an older bird new tricks.

Another way to make a formulated diet more appealing is to sprinkle the kibbles with carrot or lemon juice. Doing so changes the color, texture, and taste of the kibbles and provides some intrigue about these little pellets. You also can try enticing your cockatiel by putting a few seeds or toasted oats on top of the formulated diet. Your bird just may slip its beak into the formulated diet and find out that it's edible, too.

You also can entirely camouflage formulated diet by baking it into a cornbread mix. Cockatiels enjoy cornbread made from a mix meant for people. The mix can be customized for your cockatiel by adding pellets, grated carrot, extra egg, or greens to the basic recipe. Also consider serving formulated diet with scrambled eggs so it becomes moist.

Simple placement of food dishes plays some role in conversion as well. Your cockatiel will look in his normal seed dish for food, so that's definitely a place to put the new diet. You have probably noticed that your cockatiel has a favorite perch or other special places in his cage. You may want to put small dishes of the new diet at those locations so that your cockatiel finds the new diet wherever he goes in his cage. This tactic is certain to arouse his curiosity.

Workout

A consideration for placement of a water bowl or tube is how much exercise and creativity you want to foster in your cockatiel. Food bowls that are across the cage from water bowls encourage at least some exercise for your companion on a daily basis. If your cockatiel is an open-bowl bather, you might supply an additional, large shallow bowl on the bottom of the cage or enclosure.

Offering Treats

Even though formulated diets have the nutrients your cockatiel needs, offering a cockatiel-formulated diet, water, and absolutely nothing else isn't a good idea. Cockatiels are intelligent beings, and they appreciate the stimulation from eating foods with different colors, textures, and flavors. Offering your caged companion cockatiels a stimulating environment is one of your obligations as a pet owner. You can fulfill your commitment to exceptional pet care by providing varied treats to your cockatiels.

Treats can offer entertainment value as well as nutritional value to a cockatiel. Cockatiels love to pull apart vegetables that are made up of small pieces. They eat the centers out of juicy kernels of corn, pick the buds off broccoli florets, and dissect parsley from its stalks. Millet sprays, which are stalks of bird seed in their natural form, offer enormous entertainment. Cockatiels have limited interest in fruit, making them different from many of the parrot species kept as companion birds. Cockatiels may occasionally eat citrus, so you can offer them an orange or grapefruit rind a couple times a year. They also will occasionally try bland fruits such as pears and apples.

Preparing food for your cockatiel and devising new ways to please him with treats serves to create a bond between you and your cockatiel. He'll look forward to his treat bowl and check for what's new. And you'll have a way to express your love for your cockatiel — by preparing an interesting array of vegetables for your bird and by keeping your eyes out for new vegetables in the produce section of your supermarket.

Treats are meant to be little extra additions to a diet and a way to promote bonding between you and your cockatiel and give it added enjoyment and stimulation. A treat shouldn't upset the balance of the formulated diet you feed your bird. Treats should be low calorie and offered in small amounts. Good treats are vegetables or whole-grain products without added fat. Cockatiels like high-fat treats (so do I), but only occasionally should they be offered seeds, egg, or nuts. I guess those are the "special holiday" treats!

Veggies

The healthiest treats for your cockatiel are dark green leafy vegetables and the orange vegetables rich in vitamin A. Here are some examples:

- Broccoli
- Broccoli slaw
- Carrots
- Corn
- Dandelion
- Kale
- Leaf lettuce
- Parsley
- Spinach
- Squash
- Sweet potato
- Yams
- Zucchini

You can offer these treats in various ways. Many vegetables can be cut up, grated, sliced, or steamed. They may be served raw or cooked. You can serve some vegetables whole, too. For example, you can wedge a carrot into the bars of the cage and let your cockatiel tear it up. That's food's entertainment value! Try threading vegetables on a skewer that hangs from the cage or cut them up into a bowl. Vegetables can be very enticing if you wind them around a dangling toy or swing, attach them to the bars of a cage, or arrange them on the bottom of the cage.

If you're a busy person or don't have a lot of fresh produce on hand, you can offer frozen and even some canned vegetables to your cockatiel. Frozen peas and corn kernels thaw fast in a strainer held under hot running water. You can also serve canned corn, peas, carrots, and green beans. Another time saver is presliced packages of salad or vegetables such as broccoli slaw. Consider your cockatiel's view of food as entertainment as an excuse to try out new vegetables, new greens, and new ways of preparing and presenting food.

Grains

Foods made from grains without added sugar, salt, or oils also make good treats. Bread or toast, rice crackers, and toasted oat or puffed grain cereals are good examples. Baked crackers, cooked rice, and raw or cooked pasta are healthy, fun treats. Other ideas include breadsticks, cornbread, and warm oatmeal.

No-nos

The basic rule about feeding your cockatiel treats is that a cockatiel can eat *almost* everything you *should* eat. The rule used to be that a cockatiel can eat almost everything you eat, but humans eat a few too many things that aren't good for them. If you share some of your dinner with your cockatiel friend, that's probably fine. The "almost" in the rule is there because some people foods are harmful to cockatiels. For example, people can eat avocado with no harmful effects, but it's poisonous to your pet cockatiel.

Here's a list of foods that you should *never* feed to cockatiels:

- Alcohol
- Avocado
- Caffeine
- Chocolate

Here's are foods that you should feed only in limited amounts:

- Fat
- Salt
- Sugar

Storing Food

Bird food appeals not only to your cockatiel but also to an array of pests from seed moths to mice. Because you would prefer to save that food for your own cockatiel and not the house mouse, store the food in airtight containers. If you want to take advantage of better pricing for larger quantities of formulated diet, you can store some of it in your freezer. You can freeze rice and bean diets in ice cube trays for serving-size lumps. If you keep some seed on hand, freeze new packages for 24 hours before opening them. Doing so should kill any pests such as seed moths, which are not harmful to you or your bird but are a nuisance around the house.

Food will keep longest in cool, dry areas. If you live in a hot, humid climate, consider keeping your bird feed in the refrigerator. Watch closely for signs of mold in feed and discard the feed in a container if it does grow mold or bacteria. Cockatiels don't tolerate bad food, which can make them sick.

Cleanliness around your birds is essential. Keep lids closed on bird food containers, clean up spills when you make them, and vacuum the floor often. The best way to keep pests away is to make food unavailable to them. If you have a mouse problem, take away food bowls at night when your birds aren't eating and mice are about. Use only safe pesticides, such as pyrethrins, around your birds. Even better, use a remedy that is harmless. For example, sprinkle cayenne pepper or cinnamon in areas where ants have access to your bird cages. They are repelled by these substances.

Feeding Techniques

Feeding your bird may seem like a simple act. You get food and put it in the cockatiel's bowl. However, there are some pointers that can make feeding your bird better for your bird and easier for you. To start, don't fill your cockatiel's bowl up to the top. Your cockatiel's food will spoil before he eats all the food in the dish. Your bird will stay healthy if his food and dishes are kept clean and free from bacteria. To this end, put cockatiel feed in the bottom of a cockatiel's feed dish. The next day, empty the old food and put in new feed, again just in the bottom of the cockatiel's dish. By doing this, you aren't ever allowing mold to grow in layers of old and contaminated feed.

If the dish is soiled, wash it with soap and water and dry it, or replace it with another bowl while you wash the soiled dish at your leisure. Put in fresh vegetables on a daily basis, or more often if you live in a climate that promotes spoilage. If you serve the occasional scrambled eggs or any kind of meat, chicken, or tuna, put the food in the cage for about 15 to 20 minutes and remove what your cockatiel hasn't eaten after that time.

There's an art to scooping feed, too. Although you may be tempted to use your handy bird dishes to scoop feed out of its container, doing so contaminates the fresh feed and potentially causes the growth of bacteria. Keep some sort of scoop or cup in your feed container and use it to fill your cockatiel's dish. Doing so keeps your clean food clean.

If you feed seeds, put out fresh food every day. Cockatiels hull seeds, and their dish may look full when it is actually full of empty hulls. In between servings of new seed, you can blow the hulls off the top of the dish to expose heavier, unopened seed for your cockatiel.

Similarly, when you empty a container used for storing bird food, wash and dry it thoroughly. You don't want to leave old feed in the container when you fill it with new feed. Why? The same refrain: You're preventing the growth of mold and bacteria. All of these procedures can become habit, and you won't need to think about them anymore.

Feed your bird at the same time each day. For most bird owners, that is first thing in the morning. Cockatiels wake up hungry and active. Their natural activity level is fairly low during the day, and they become vocal in the evening before settling in to roost. Water is an important part of feeding your cockatiel. Check that your bird's water is clean throughout the day, and do the same for its feed dishes. While you're at it, run the vacuum or sweep around your buddy's cage. Take vegetable treats out of your cockatiel's cage before they spoil.

Chapter 5

Getting Things for Your Cockatiel

. . . .

In This Chapter

▶ Providing perches for your birds

▶ Offering sources of calcium

▶ Choosing the right toys

▶ Covering up the cage

▶ Stocking up on stuff to make your life easier

. . . .

You have the responsibility of providing your captive companions with the best living conditions you can provide. What does that involve? Well, cockatiels love to play, so providing toys for your cockatiel gives her things to do and keeps her curious brain active. Providing branches as perches can keep her feet in good shape, and fastening a cuttlebone to a cage provides a source of calcium. Besides the items your cockatiel needs to be happy and healthy, you can purchase all sorts of accessories that make your life easier as you clean and organize your cockatiel's environment. That's what this chapter is all about.

Dangling, Clipping, and Threading Food for Your Cockatiel

Much of what you provide your cockatiels for refreshment and nourishment should be served in bowls. This elevates food, treats, and water off the floor for the sake of cleanliness. But you have other options. You can twist greens through cage bars, twirl a carrot onto a wire grid, or spear firm veggies with a rod to hold them up off the floor and offer them at a cockatiel's eye level. If you have a finicky cockatiel, these are good ways to entice her to try fresh food.

Clips and holders are available to hold vegetables and treats onto a cage. Special spiral holders are meant to hold dried heads of millet spray. Clips or nuts and bolts hold cuttlebones. Broccoli florets can be planted perfectly between the bars of a cage. You can use an old-fashioned wooden peg clothespin to attach sprigs of parsley or a cuttlebone to a cage. The clothespins become safe toys as well!

Use only wooden peg clothespins to clip food to a cage. The spring mechanism in other clothespins may be dangerous.

There's no reason your cockatiel should like any certain color better than others, so you can decorate to go with your own décor. With some bigger birds or the feistiest cockatiels, you may need to look for a style of bowl that can't be tipped over.

Perches

If you think about it, your cockatiel is always on her feet. Does she ever kick back and relax? Put her feet up? Well, maybe one foot at a time! Many cages come with a set of wooden dowel perches, which look pretty and uniform in the store. The well-being of your cockatiel's feet requires a variety of shapes of perching surfaces. She is less likely to develop foot problems if she can hold her feet in different positions.

You may offer your bird comfortable footing by changing some of the perches in a cage to wooden dowel perches of different sizes and shapes. Oval is a good, smooth shape. As a guide, your cockatiel's toes shouldn't wrap all the way around a perch, but the perch shouldn't be so large that the cockatiel can't hold on well.

Natural perches (The concept should gnaw at you)

Use natural branches in your cages (see Figure 5-1). They offer the added benefit of not being the same diameter along the entire length of the perch. Natural branches serve another purpose: Cockatiels entertain themselves for hours by chewing on their perches and stripping the bark industriously when you first place them in their cages. If you live in an area where eucalyptus grows, you can offer fresh branches to your companion cockatiels as a little bit of their Australian homeland too. Your cockatiels don't enjoy only the branches; they also chew the leaves for entertainment. You also can offer other types of leafed branches as perches, which your cockatiels will messily customize to suit themselves.

Figure 5-1:
Choose natural branches over dowels for your cockatiel's perches.

Most fruit wood can be used for perches safely, but not cherry wood, which is poisonous. Avoid sappy pine branches in choosing cage furniture. Manzanita branches are available through catalogs and in pet shops. Manzanita is a hard wood that birds can't chew, so it stays beautiful for a long time. But don't be tempted to use all manzanita perches. Chewing on branches and bark is a good diversion for your cockatiels.

Other branches you can safely offer include willow, oak, maple, and birch. Most of the fruit woods make excellent perches, as long as they haven't been sprayed with pesticides. Wash off tree branches thoroughly before being offering them to your cockatiel. You can bake eucalyptus branches on low for an hour or so before "serving" them to your cockatiels. Doing so makes the whole house smell like you're cooking cough syrup! Don't try microwaving your branches. They won't fit so well, and I can't offer you appropriate cooking times for killing germs without cooking the sticks to charcoal.

Here are safe, natural branches to use as perches:

- Apple
- Citrus
- Eucalyptus
- Grapevine
- Hedge
- Manzanita
- Maple
- Oak
- Willow

Other fun perches

In addition to natural branches, plastic (or PVC) and rope perches are available for your cockatiel. Choose perches that are safe. For example, PVC perches should have grooves or scoring in them so that they're not slippery. Acrylic perches come with either a rough finish that is frosty-looking or a smooth finish. One of these hard perches of man-made materials should not be the only perch you offer a cockatiel. Cement perches may help keep nails trimmed, and they're naturally rough, offering a steady perch for your cockatiel. They are hard, however, so be sure to include a few branches in the cage as well. You don't enjoy standing all day on hard surfaces, and neither does your cockatiel.

None of these hard materials offer opportunities for chewing, which you can supply in other ways and by offering a variety of perches. Rope perches can fray as a cockatiel picks at them, so you may want to let your cockatiel use them only during supervised play time. That way, if she gets caught in the loose string, you can come to her aid. Offering a variety of furniture is a good idea, as is occasional redecorating!

Grit (Just Say No)

For many years, a bowl of grit was a standard bird cage furnishing as it was believed to be necessary for digestion in birds. Grit for birds basically consists of small particles of sand or stone. Pass up this item on the grocery store or pet store shelf. It has been proven that cockatiels do not need grit to aid in the digestion of their food. In fact, some cockatiels, when ill, eat too much grit and their digestive process becomes clogged by it.

Cuttlebone and Mineral Blocks

Cuttlebone, a source of calcium for your cockatiels, is not the most attractive part of cage furnishings, but it does provide a nutritional benefit. Just like the milk we drank as youngsters, it helps your cockatiel build strong bones. A cuttlebone is an oblong-shaped white object about one-quarter inch thick. It's a piece of a marine animal, the cuttlefish. One side is hard and you should hang the hard side against the cage. That allows your cockatiel to chew on the soft side. Your cockatiel will probably ignore a cuttlebone most of the time. She will perch on the cuttlebone, nibble on it occasionally, and generally get used to it as a fixture in the cage. Then, when she needs a boost of calcium, cuttlebone will disappear quickly. Breeding birds devour cuttlebone when they're preparing to have eggs. Pet cockatiels usually chew cuttlebone when they're molting and are growing in strong, shiny new feathers. Pet cockatiels do sometimes lay eggs, so they may need the calcium in a cuttlebone for that reason as well. Replace the cuttlebone when it becomes soiled.

Cuttlebone is a flotation device on cuttlefish, which are relatives of squid and live in many parts of the world's oceans, except around North America. They propel themselves with jet propulsion, can produce inky screens like an octopus, and catch food with tentacles. They have the ability to change color to some degree in order to blend in with their environment during their short life span. Check them out if you ever visit the Monterey Bay Aquarium in Monterey, California.

Homemade mineral blocks

To make homemade mineral blocks, you need the following ingredients:

- 2 parts plaster of Paris
- 5 parts powdered lime (garden lime)
- 4 parts bone meal
- 1 part mineral supplement

Mix with water until you have a smooth, heavy, gravy consistency. Mold in a plastic cup or similar container of desired size. Insert u-shaped tie wire with the ends sticking out 2 or 3 inches. Allow to harden (which may take 2 to 3 days).

If you want to offer your cockatiel its calcium in a neater form, you can place a mineral block in her home. Their basic ingredient is plaster of Paris, some with coloring, flavoring, or grit added. You can even make your own (see the sidebar "Homemade mineral blocks").

Aberrant forms of calcium may become attractive to your cockatiel if you don't offer any in her cage. Your cockatiel may become fascinated with chalk or decide to create holes in sheet rock walls. It's easier to provide a cuttle-bone or a mineral block.

Adding a Little Color

Birds can see colors, unlike our canine and feline pets, so they enjoy colorful cage accessories. As your cockatiel's provider and interior decorator, you can provide this color by giving your cockatiel some fun toys. Cockatiels are curious, playful birds who enjoy the diversion that toys offer.

Here are some qualities to look for in toys for cockatiels:

- Color
- Movable parts
- Wood to chew
- Leather to chew
- Dangly parts
- Beads to move
- Knots to untie
- Variety in shapes
- Toy doubling as a perch
- Unbreakable mirror

Beyond beauty, cockatiel toys need to be safe. They should be made for birds the size of cockatiels and should be made of safe materials. Smaller toys made for budgies can too easily be dismantled by a cockatiel. Toy hangers should be stainless steel. S-hook and key-ring clasps can become dangerous. Threads or loops can also be dangerous, unless you're supervising your bird. Leather should be vegetable-tanned, and coloring should be nontoxic.

As your cockatiel's interior decorator, you can add variety to the cage by planning for changes in the wall art! You may buy new toys on a regular basis to keep your cockatiel stimulated. You can also accomplish the same thing by cycling and recycling toys on a regular basis. When you bring out a toy that has been in retirement for a week or two, it becomes newly fascinating to a cockatiel. That's easier on your budget than constantly buying new toys!

A mirror is a perfect cage toy. The cockatiel in the mirror becomes a "friend" for a single cockatiel. If you have a male cockatiel, he will usually whistle and talk to that friend (or rival?) and provide you with hours of entertainment. Most cockatiels love swings, which can be made of a variety of materials. Birds love chewing the wood and leather from well-made colorful toys such as those available from Birds of Play. They untie the knots from their leather toys, unstring the beads, and chew off colored shapes from their toys. Which is exactly the kind of activity for which you get a toy! Most bird toys are meant to be destroyed. Bell Plastics makes practically indestructible, colorful perches, play stands and foot toys that will keep both you and your cockatiel entertained.

Our cockatiels are smart, inquisitive animals. The main reason for giving them toys is to provide them with something to do and something to keep their smart brain cells stimulated. For more toy inspiration, order a catalog from one of the established bird catalogs like Pet Bird Xpress, Hornbeck's, or Pet Warehouse.

A Cover-Up Operation

Should you cover your cockatiel at night? You can decide. Regulating the downtime in your cockatiel's schedule certainly has its benefits. For example, cockatiels don't understand the difference between a weekday and a weekend morning, so a covered cockatiel stays quiet longer, allowing you to sleep in longer — although maybe not as late as you'd like! Usually a cockatiel gets restless as the morning progresses and she figures out that breakfast time has come and gone.

A cover is also a means of controlling the number of hours a cockatiel is awake. If a cockatiel has long hours because she stays up to watch the late show with you and then gets up early when the kids are getting ready for school, that could very well be a stimulus to its hormones. She will think conditions are right for laying eggs or will start to set up a spot for nesting. You won't be too welcome in that spot. Using a cover to give a cockatiel 10- to 12-hour days instead of edging up to 15-hour days is one way to keep hormonal behavior under control.

You can find many things around the house to use as cage covers, including sheets, towels, and baby receiving blankets (see Figure 5-2). Heavier materials and darker colors block out more light, especially if you're serious about sleeping in on the weekends. You can also make your own cage cover and let your creative juices run wild in the process. You may want to monogram it, decorate it with moon and star shapes, stitch cartoons on it, or applique it with cockatiels.

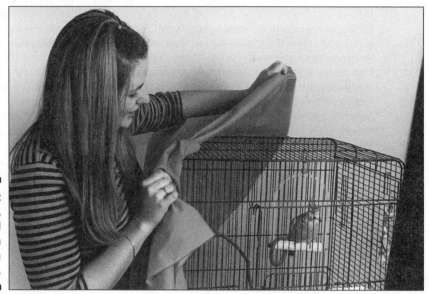

Figure 5-2:
A blanket, towel, or old sheet can serve as a cage cover.

During the day, you can use your cage cover as a feed guard. Hang it over one side of the cage to retain some of the food and treats that cockatiels throw about during their normal eating and playtime activities.

Items That Make Your Life Easier

Cockatiels are cuddly pets with cheery whistles. They are companions who can brighten your day. But owning cockatiels means cleaning cages, wiping splatters of food off your walls, and vacuuming feed and feathers from your floors. Some conveniences, however, can make life easier for both of you.

Splat! Some food or waste hits the floor on a regular basis with a cockatiel in the house. It doesn't need to hit the floor, though. Though mottled green and brown carpeting may be the solution for a room housing a cockatiel, it may not be the most attractive solution. A perfect bird room has easy-to-clean linoleum. If you have a carpeted home or apartment, place a large plastic office mat under your bird cages. The mat can be swept and then wiped clean, saving the carpeting and the cleaning deposit. You can also put washable towels or sheets under cages. When cockatiels are out of their cages, newspapers can catch droppings. You'll quickly figure out where the favorite roosting places are.

You may want to hang sheets on the walls around your bird cages. Sheets can be washed and come in many attractive prints. I don't recommend the solid colors, as they won't be solid for long. Alternatively, you can hang shower curtains behind your bird cages. They conveniently come with holes in them, and you can find wall-mount hooks to accommodate them perfectly. Shower curtains can be wiped clean or replaced easily and inexpensively if need be.

Wide, thick plastic is another wall covering to consider. You also can put up bamboo screening. Your birds will love customizing the bamboo as they chew on it, and it will keep them entertained for months. You can always leave a wall bare and paint it with a high- gloss, easily washable paint. Plan to wipe it down daily and repaint every so often. Maybe you're lucky enough to have a neat cockatiel. They may exist out there — every cockatiel is an individual, after all.

Keep a broom and vacuum cleaner near your bird cages. A little portable, hand-held vacuum isn't a bad idea, either. If you don't allow your cockatiel's area to become messy, it won't be the least bit attractive to a mouse or other roving scavenger. If you have only one pet cockatiel, maybe you aren't anticipating much of a mess. Let's hope you're right.

Bins, Receptacles, and Drawers

It's amazing how many things you need to store near a bird cage. The most convenient place to store them is near the location where you'll use them. Arrange for storage tubs, drawer space, or closet space near your bird cage.

You'll probably have these items to store near a bird cage:

- Bird books
- Bird playgrounds
- Broom
- Feed
- First aid kit
- Garbage bags

✔ Grooming supplies

✔ Papers or cage liners

✔ Towel for restraining cockatiel

✔ Toys

✔ Travel cage or carrier

✔ Treats

✔ Vacuum cleaner

✔ Wastebasket

As long as you've committed to looking after your feathered wonder, you may as well make it easy. Spend your energy devising games to play with your cockatiel and running out to bird stores for the latest toys. That's much more fun than hunting down cleaning equipment or not being able to locate styptic powder when your cockatiel is bleeding. With everything so organized, you may be tempted to whistle while you work. In the company of cockatiels, you're likely to get a whistle back, too.

Chapter 6

Trimming and Grooming

. . . .

In This Chapter

▶ Gathering your grooming tools

▶ Finding out how to hold a cockatiel safely

▶ Discovering out how and when to trim wing feathers and nails

▶ Steering clear of the beak

. . . .

*E*very day, you take time to brush your hair, brush and floss your teeth, and you occasionally trim your nails. Or at least I hope you do. You're more socially acceptable if you do. Cockatiels need occasional grooming as well. They groom those precious feathers on a daily if not an hourly basis. After all, cockatiels depend on their feathers to keep them warm and water-proof, and to help them look attractive to members of the opposite sex.

What's more, your cockatiel needs help keeping her nails trimmed and wing feathers trimmed. With this chapter, you can perform your bird's grooming yourself. If you're nervous about tackling this task, you can rely on the services of a professional. Even if you do decide to groom your cockatiel your-self, have an experienced bird groomer show you what to do the first time. Professionals who can groom your bird or show you how to do it include bird breeders, avian veterinarians, some pet store staff, and mobile bird groomers.

Assembling the Right Tools

You need some special tools to trim wings and nails when you're getting ready for bird grooming, but most of them are readily available. You may already have them around your house or can find them at a drugstore.

"Software" for bird grooming

The first tool is your software. No, I'm not talking about the step-by-step instructions that you find on a CD or in your computer. I'm referring to a soft, clean towel to restrain your cockatiel. (I describe how to use the towel later in this chapter.) If the grooming process upsets your cockatiel, then she will have something else to chomp down on besides your hand or fingers. If you have an assistant to help you with the grooming, one person can hold the cockatiel, and the second person can do the clipping and trimming.

Cockatiels are small birds, so it's very possible to do all their grooming yourself, without an assistant — after someone has shown you how. Some owners prefer to have someone else do the grooming so that their cockatiel doesn't associate the restraint and stress of grooming with the trusted owner. Other owners have built a high level of trust in their birds and have taught them to accept restraint and inspection as well as behaviors such as hopping on their finger. These trusting cockatiels won't necessarily like grooming, but they won't bite and can be handled without a towel.

No bloodshed in bird grooming

When trimming your bird's nails, you may accidentally clip a nail too short, causing it to bleed. Contrary to popular belief, a cockatiel will not bleed to death quickly. Still, you don't want to leave your companion cockatiel in distress, and stopping the blood flow is important for his well being. Several items are available to help stop the bleeding.

Styptic powder, which is certainly familiar to men who shave with razors, is invaluable as a way to control bleeding. It comes packaged as a bitter-tasting gold-colored powder, just for birds. You'll find styptic powder for birds at pet supply stores, and as one of the products available in avian first aid kits. It is the same product as a human being would use, so a pharmacist can help you find some.

In a pinch, you can use other substances to stop the bleeding. The first is a bar of soap. (You now have a use for the hotel soaps you've been collecting in your travels.) Hold the bird's nail in the bar of soap. The constant application of pressure will staunch the flow of blood. You also can use two cooking ingredients to stop the cut from bleeding: cornstarch and flour. Simply apply one of them to the bleeding nail. When you're getting ready to groom your cockatiel's nails, have one of these items on hand.

Look sharp!

The scissors you use to trim your cockatiel's wing feathers should be sharp. You don't want to hack off feathers. You want to clip them precisely and cleanly, one by one. Any pair of scissors you have at home will work, the important thing is that they are sharp. Get good quality scissors from an office supply store or scissors meant to cut out fabric from a sewing store. Hair cutting scissors from a beauty store or dog grooming scissors in a pet store are other choices. You probably won't find bird grooming scissors anywhere. You may want to dedicate a pair of scissors to your bird grooming for the sake for sanitation.

Your nail implements also need to be sharp. You'll be using tools made for people to groom your cockatiel's nails. You can use human nail clippers, nail scissors, and even a file. Professional groomers may use a Dremel drill, which you can find at the hardware store. Leave this tool to the professionals though, as a slip can cause a lot of harm in inexperienced hands. You shouldn't be surprised when your veterinarian or a bird groomer uses a drill, however.

Deciding When to Clip

So how do you know when your cockatiel is due for a feather or nail trim?

Here's how you know that it's time to clip your cockatiel's wing feathers:

- ✔ When your friend is gliding about the room easily. That may mean there's only one grown-out feather on each wing to trim, but that's all it takes for a cockatiel to have a great deal of airlift.

- ✔ When your cockatiel is at the end of one of her twice-a-year molts. She will have grown in new wing feathers. If you haven't noticed, she may not have noticed, either. But eventually she'll discover that she has the power of flight back again.

- ✔ When your male cockatiel is being uppity with you. He can reach high heights and look down on you, but you can't reach him. He's snappy and controlling. Clipping his wings will make him rely on you again for transportation and will soften his tone.

- ✔ If you just got your cockatiel and the bird's feathers have never been trimmed. You'll develop the closest relationship with your bird if she is easy for you to control and if she needs you. With clipped wings, she does need you to get off the floor and up to safer heights. She also needs you to go from room to room. When she needs to go somewhere, you're the one who can get her there. She just has to figure out how to ask. That fosters trust and communication, especially when each of you is successfully getting your points across.

Feathers grow in over a six-week period. If you trim wings in the middle, you or your bird groomer will have to skip feathers that are just growing in, as they have nerves and a blood supply. You can't cut them without hurting your cockatiel. So, when that feather grows in, it will need to be trimmed back.

You should clip your bird's nails on an as-needed basis, but here's how you know for sure when it's time for a trim:

✔ If the youngest and oldest members of the family can't hold the family pet without getting scratched or bruised. Their skin is the most sensitive, and holding a cockatiel may be painful for these members of the family unless her nails are clipped.

Young cockatiels and handicapped cockatiels need to have fairly sharp nails in order to get a good footing. If a person with sensitive skin needs to handle a young cockatiel, urge her to pull down her shirt sleeve so that she isn't injured by the bird's sharp nails.

✔ If the nails are getting snagged in your sweaters or in your carpeting. They're just too long for the cockatiel's own safety.

✔ If an errant nail is getting long and threatens to grow up into the pad of your cockatiel's foot. Your cockatiel never kicks back and puts her feet up, so her feet need to be in excellent shape. If a long toenail or two threatens her comfort, then it's time to take care of those nails.

✔ If you can see visually that they are too long. When she perches, they wrap around each other. When she walks on a flat surface, they force her feet up off the surface.

✔ If your cockatiel has a foot injury or defect that prevents her from perching normally. Without wear and perching, her nails may grow too long.

Holding Your Cockatiel

You need to hold your cockatiel in order to groom her, and there are ways to do this that are safe for both for you and your cockatiel. A sweet, trusting, tame cockatiel who is used to handling is a pleasure to groom. She will be uncomfortable but tolerant of the procedure and won't put the groomer in danger of being bitten.

When restraining a cockatiel, do not compress its breast. A cockatiel can't breathe if you do that because she doesn't have a diaphragm to do the work of expanding and contracting her chest like humans do.

Don't try either method of grooming described in this section without instruction from an experienced bird groomer.

Using a towel and a helper

If you need to use a towel to groom your cockatiel, then you need a helper. You can immobilize your cockatiel in a towel, holding her from the back around her neck (see Figure 6-1). Support her back with the palm of your hand, and hold on to her feet or let her grasp them. Leave the front of the towel open.

Cockatiels come in many colors, including gray (or normal) pearl shown here.

These gray-pied and cinnamon-pied cockatiels illustrate the striking color and pattern combinations that are available.

This is a female cinnamon cockatiel. A male would have a bright-yellow head.

Lutino cockatiels are mostly white to cream or yellow.

The lack of red cheek patches is a mutation in this cockatiel hen.

Albino cockatiels have no pigment, which means no cheek patches. They have red eyes with a pink beak and feet.

Normal gray cockatiels. The male has a yellow head and black feathers under his tail. The hen is more subdued in coloring.

Lutino cockatiels have the same markings to differentiate sexes. A hen still has striped feathers under her tail; a male has solid-colored feathers.

This gray pearl-pied cockatiel is sampling seeds.

If your cockatiel is joining you for a meal, it can eat almost anything that you *should*. No junk food!

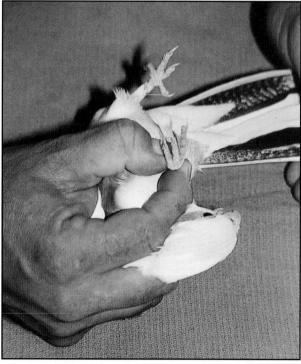

When restraining a cockatiel for grooming, hold him with your fingers firmly but gently around his neck and jowls. Don't restrain his chest.

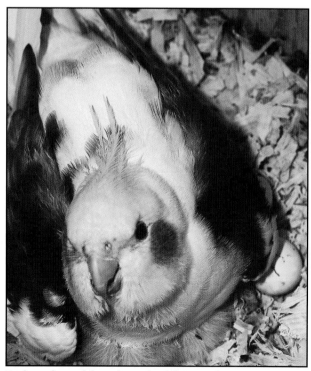

Both male and female cockatiels care for eggs and chicks.

Cockatiel chicks have faces only a mother could love.

As cockatiel chicks mature, their feathers come in as pin feathers.

Cockatiel chicks grow rapidly in their first four weeks of life.

Natural perches are best for your cockatiel's feet.

Cockatiels love to hang out around plants such as ficus, succulents, and ferns.

Cockatiels enjoy the freedom of an outside aviary.

Cockatiels benefit from exposure to natural light.

This female gray pearl is perching quietly outside her cage.

You can get your cockatiel a "pet" of its own, like this canary.

These two males are having a disagreement. Notice their slicked-back crests, which indicates aggression.

Cockatiels can yawn, believe it or not.

Cinnamon pearl and gray pearl cockatiels having a mild disagreement.

Figure 6-1:
Using a
towel to
secure a
cockatiel.

To trim your cockatiel's wings or nails while holding her in this fashion, prop her gently on a solid surface such as a table, trying to make her feel secure. The cockatiel handler should gently pull out one wing, then the other, and then one foot at a time. If your cockatiel lashes out with her beak, give her some towel to chew. In an attempt to convince the bird to blame the experience on "Mr. Towel" instead of on one of the people involved, some people make a big deal out of tossing the towel to the floor and chastising it. It never hurts to try!

You can't leave your cockatiel wrapped up like a burrito for long periods of time, especially on hot days, because she'll quickly overheat. If your cockatiel is panting and holding her wings out to the side when released from the towel, spray or mist her with water to cool her off. Concentrate on wetting her feet and the area under her wings.

Flying solo

You can use a similar restraint when clipping wings and nails on your own. You'll have the best luck with a friendly cockatiel. To clip the first wing, hold her with your first two fingers around her neck, pressing on her cheekbones to keep her from turning her head (see Figure 6-2). Support her with the palm of your hand. With the other hand, clip the wing feathers one at a time, checking for blood feathers as you go and avoiding those. (A *blood feather* is a feather that is still growing in.) Turn the bird around so she's resting on your chest, pull out her other wing, and clip it. Molting and blood feathers are discussed in Chapter 7.

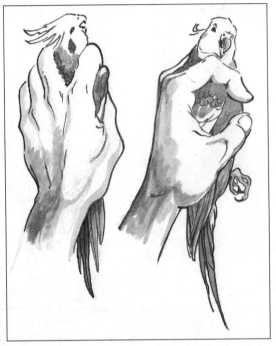

Figure 6-2:
The right way to hold a cockatiel if you're not using a towel.

To clip her nails, hold her again around the neck with one hand, using some of those fingers to pull out a leg so you can clip the very tip of each nail. This maneuver probably depends on having hands and cockatiels that are just the right size for each other. If you're having difficulty holding a bird on your own, get a helper for this job.

Trimming Wing Feathers

You can give your cockatiel varying amounts of flight capability depending on the amount of feathers you clip on her wings. With cockatiel chicks who haven't mastered flying, it's a good idea to gradually clip their wings. Cockatiels who learn to fly, land, and use their bodies to move about a cage are more sure of themselves when they've lost the ability to fly. For this reason, start by clipping just the two outer flight feathers on each wing of a cockatiel who is just learning to fly. The cockatiel will be slowed down but will still fly quite well. About a week later, clip the next two feathers. The next week, clip the next two feathers, and so on. With this schedule, by the time a cockatiel is grounded, she will have gradually lost the ability to fly and gotten progressively better at controlling her mobility. She'll still confidently hop about a cage and will know how to land. Ideally a breeder will use this method of clipping before you ever get your bird. You can give your own bird the chance to learn about flying at any age, though, by letting her wings grow back and gradually clipping them back in this way.

WARNING

Cockatiels who are clipped as very young chicks, before they attain motor skills and know how to handle their bodies to fly and land, often "crash land" and break their tail feathers or hurt themselves.

REMEMBER

When trimming a cockatiel's wing feathers, be sure to do a symmetrical job, trimming both wings an equal amount. Your cockatiel not only will look good but, more importantly, will be balanced when she flies or sails along. You don't want to make her clumsy.

How often to clip

When deciding how much to clip your cockatiel's wings, consider her environment. If she lives in an aviary with a safety area, then flight is permissible for her, and she'll get lots of exercise. If you plan to enter your cockatiel in exhibitions, the judges will consider her total confirmation, so you'll want to show her with unclipped wings. If your cockatiel lives in the company of cats and dogs and you want to be sure that she can escape from them, you may want to leave her some flight capability. If you want to allow your cockatiel to fly in the house, but slow enough that she's not likely to hurt herself, leave more of her wings unclipped. If your cockatiel may be able to get outside, or could go through a window or door in your home because they're often open, you probably want to give her the most severe clip. If you have a bossy, dominant male cockatiel, a fairly severe wing clip will change his attitude. If you're just getting to know a new, older cockatiel, clip rather severely also. A severe wing clip will help you to work with an older cockatiel, as she'll be more dependent on you to help her get around. If you need to chase after her, you won't have to go as far, either! She also won't hurt herself in any mad flights about unfamiliar territory.

What to clip

Don't clip more than 10 primary feathers from a cockatiel's wings (see Figure 6-3). If you want to give your cockatiel some ability to fly, clip fewer feathers or clip the feathers farther down, merely shortening them. Your cockatiel will still need to have wing exercise, especially with clipped feathers. Take some time every day to hold her feet and encourage her to flap. Chances are good she'll develop some strong chest muscles by using what wing feathers she has to get around. It really isn't possible to ground a cockatiel. You'll be surprised how well your clipped cockatiel can get around.

Figure 6-3:
These are the wing feathers to clip.

Even with ten primary flight feathers clipped from each wing, don't risk taking your cockatiel outside on your shoulder. She may get scared by a dog, cat, or car and fly into danger. If you want your cockatiel to be outside in the sunshine, take her out in a carrying cage or train her to use a bird harness and leash.

Clip a cockatiel's wing feathers one by one, after you've decided how many to clip and whether to clip them to the level of the coverts or to leave them longer. Before trimming a wing feather, examine it to see whether it's a blood feather. Don't clip blood feathers, because doing so will cause your bird to bleed. Its tip may be feathered out, but at the base, it still has nerves and blood vessels. If you clip the feather at this level, the bird will bleed and be in pain. A blood feather siphons blood, and sometimes the only way to stop the flow is to pull out that shaft.

If you injure a blood feather, or if your cockatiel injures one, you will probably need to pull out the feather shaft to stop it from bleeding. A veterinarian may need to do this for you. The shaft needs to be pulled out with a firm hold, a quick movement, and while the cockatiel's wing bones are supported. Don't balk at seeking professional help from an avian veterinarian.

Don't leave stray long feathers when you clip your cockatiel's wings. Cockatiel feathers are meant to grow together, and they support each other when they grow in, during the vulnerable blood feather stage. A long feather at the tip of each wing may get caught in cage bars or entangled in toys. Leaving a stray long feather in your cockatiel's wing increases her chance of injury or accident.

Trimming Nails

You can be as sneaky or as straightforward as you want about trimming your cockatiel's toenails. You can do the job yourself or can have someone else do it. Probably the first item to consider is whether you even want to clip your cockatiel's toenails at all.

Consider both the dexterity and precision necessary to hold or clip nails. Wear your glasses if you need them for close work. If you have trouble working a nail clipper or a pair of scissors, then get help for the task. This is one job that you don't want to botch.

To cut or not to cut

Normal, healthy cockatiels wear their nails down through daily perching and preening. At certain times of the year, their nails are growing and may feel sharp to you, but you'll notice that in a few weeks their sharp tips are worn down to normal again.

Young cockatiels may have sharp toenails. They're new and haven't been worn down yet. But don't clip their nails just yet. The chick is learning to fly and land and needs the gripping power of her sharp nails to hang onto the unexpected landing pads she creates in her flying adventures. She also needs them to hold onto perches and crawl about the cage in the clumsy fashion that chicks do.

What to cut and how to cut

There are sneaky ways to make sure that your cockatiel's nails don't puncture your sensitive skin. One is to have clippers ready when she's hanging on her cage. As you can, clip the tip of the nails. No restraint, no fuss, and no pain. Another way is to teach your cockatiel to give you her foot, either through the cage bars or while she's relaxing with you (see Figure 6-4). Then use a file to keep the points of her nails filed. Filing could become a habit for both of you, making grooming pretty painless.

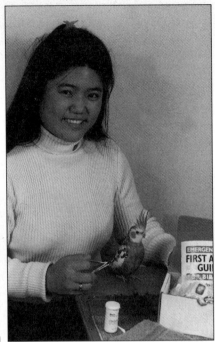

Figure 6-4:
This cockatiel is about to politely offer his foot for a nail trimming.

Cockatiels have blood vessels at the base of their nails. They also need some climbing and perching ability with those nails of theirs. For their comfort and yours, clip only the tip of a toenail. You can be the most sure of yourself when clipping a light-colored cockatiel. Their nails are white, and you can see the blood vessels at the base of the nail.

Off Limits: The Beak of a Bird

Trimming a bird's beak is not a job for a bird owner. It's a job for a professional. Normally, cockatiels keep their own beaks trimmed by chewing, eating their food, and wiping their beak on hard surfaces. They don't need a beak trim their whole lives. Many of the reasons for beak overgrowth are caused by a bird's health, so an avian veterinarian really needs to see these birds to figure out why a cockatiel's beak is growing extra-long or extra-fast. The cause could be as serious as a case of beak and feather disease, or the problem may stem from a parasite invasion, the cockatiel's diet, or liver disease.

Beaks have horny, keratin tips, but near their bases, they're alive with nerves and growing tissue. An amateur clipping a beak may hurt some of the sensitive part of the beak. And treating beak overgrowth cosmetically may only mask a more serious health problem.

Chapter 7

Freedom! Time Outside the Cage

· ·

In This Chapter

▶ Birdproofing your home

▶ Playing your time away

▶ Finding out how to pet your pet

▶ Snapping a picture of your birdie

▶ Finding an escaped bird

· ·

A cockatiel needs to spend time out of his cage daily. He needs the added exercise of pattering around your table and climbing the curtains. A cockatiel is a flock animal, so letting your bird out of his cage gives him the chance to interact with his flock. Your cockatiel will love the time you can spend with him either cuddling or playing a game. Cockatiels will generally allow themselves to be touched in certain places, love to be scratched in special places, and resent some other handling. You want to make friends with your cockatiel, so scratching him where it itches is the way to go.

You'll love the cockatiel version of fetch. Guess who gets to chase the ball? You. You and your cockatiel can play other games and have other interactions that enforce your bond. Though not up to chess or a card game, a cockatiel is clever enough to go on rides, learn a few tricks, and teach you a thing or two about coming when you're called.

While your gorgeous cockatiel is out of his cage, don't forget about the photo opportunities. Your cockatiel may want his own Web page, so you need pictures. You also want a photo for your wallet so that you can show your bird's breeder what a talented, gorgeous creature is in your life thanks to him. There are always photo contests to enter, too. Stand up for cockatiel rights! They're family pets, too. Don't let the dogs take all the pet photo contest awards. And keep those owners of tropical rainforest birds on their toes by showing them how truly gorgeous and clever a cockatiel can be.

Making Your Home Bird-Safe

From the perspective of a bird, the average home or apartment offers plenty of things to get into. Just as you'd childproof a home when expecting a toddler to visit, you should make your home bird-safe on those occasions when your cockatiel is out and about. You may need to think twice before doing some household tasks, such as spraying for bugs, or before applying hairspray. Think of your cockatiel and its formidable respiratory system, which also makes him vulnerable to fumes, smoke, and chemicals, before you perform any task that may harm your bird. If you still must fumigate or spray or style your hair, make sure that your bird is nowhere near. Sometimes that may mean sending him away for a few days while you clean your oven or spray for fleas.

Your cockatiel benefits from exposure to new experiences. He will be more accepting of new situations and less rigid about change if he has a variety of experiences that eventually become part of his normal routine. For that reason, and also to prevent a cockatiel from frequently screaming for your attention, get in the habit of taking a cockatiel from room to room with you when you're home. Your cockatiel doesn't need constant attention during these excursions. You have work to do, too!

Your cockatiel appreciates just being near you. Teach him to play on a stand or to stay in a particular spot in each room you frequent. You can get a cockatiel playgym, turn a chair into a bird stand by laying papers under it in strategic places, let your cockatiel play on a towel bar while you shower, or give the top of an end table to your cockatiel as his own. At first you'll need to teach him that he shouldn't wander. Every time he ventures from his designated area, put him back right away. Be persistent. If he figures out that you give up, he'll invent a game that wears you out so that he can get his way.

Your cockatiel can join you in any activities that don't involve fumes and chemicals. She may like a snack while you two spend time together. Serve a few toasted oats or a sprig of parsley to maximize her experience. Beware! House plants, lamps, and windowsills are at risk if you choose play locations near or on them.

Windows and mirrors

A cockatiel who's flying in your house for the first time won't know what the windows and mirrors are. From her perspective, they're openings to more space for free flight. To avoid an accident, if not the ultimate catastrophe, draw your curtains, close the blinds, and cover large mirrors with a towel. Get in the habit of doing this. Eventually a smart cockatiel will learn where his boundaries are and may learn to avoid your windows and mirrors. If this isn't the case with your bird, then continue letting her out to play only when the room is ready for her.

The kitchen

There really isn't any reason for your cockatiel to be in the kitchen with you. He would be in mortal danger from the pots of boiling water, hot surfaces, dishpans of water, and poisonous substances to chew on. And you certainly don't welcome her dust or feathers — or droppings — around your food. This is one room of the house that is not even an option for a location for your cockatiel's cage or for the company of feathered friends.

You may have a deadly poison in your kitchen. When nonstick cookware and bakeware are overheated, they release a toxin that is deadly to birds — within minutes. This danger is nothing to take lightly, and the toxins kills many families of birds every year. You shouldn't have these type of pots in your home. If you do choose to keep a nonstick pan and it boils dry or starts to overheat, open windows and quickly remove birds from the area.

Harmful fumes

Coal miners took canaries with them into the mines for a reason. The canaries felt the effects of poisonous gas before miners did, warning them of an invisible danger. Many cosmetic and cleaning substances have the same effect on your cockatiel. Smoke does, too. Here are some things that can be dangerous to birds:

- Aerosol sprays
- Smoke, including cigarette smoke
- Cleaners
- Hair spray
- Natural gas leak
- New carpeting
- Pesticides
- Room fresheners
- Rug cleaner
- Scented candles
- Self-cleaning oven

Plants

Including fresh greens in a cockatiel's diet is a good idea, but it's not necessarily good for those greens to consist of a steady diet of your houseplants.

Some houseplants don't have an ill effect, but others are known to be poisonous. You can safely keep ficus, ferns, succulents, and palms around your cockatiels. Philodendron and diffenbachia, however, are houseplants that are known to be poisonous to cockatiels. Popular Christmas plants that can make your cockatiel ill are poinsettia, holly, and mistletoe. Consider other decorating schemes for the holidays.

If your cockatiel eats something poisonous, get help fast and stay calm! Many communities have emergency veterinary clinics. Does your avian veterinarian have an emergency number to call after hours? Either is the best recourse if your cockatiel has an extreme reaction to a poison. There is also a national poison hotline run by the American Society for the Prevention of Cruelty to Animals (ASPCA). There is a charge for services, so have a charge card ready when you call. You can reach the ASPCA-run National Animal Poison Control Center at 1-800-548-2423 or 1-888-4ANIHELP (1-888-426-4435).

If you're getting help for your cockatiel, you need to know some things. First, what did the cockatiel eat? Get a sample to take with you if you're going to the veterinarian. Take the cage lining, or the cockatiel's cage if there are unusual droppings or the bird is vomiting. If your cockatiel ate something that comes in a bottle or breathed a noxious fume, take the bottle of offending poison with you or have it ready if you'll be on the phone with poison control. Be very observant. Let your medical aid know when the poison was ingested or breathed, when the bird started showing symptoms, what those symptoms are, and how your cockatiel is behaving now.

Bodies of water

Your cockatiel would be in danger if he were flying into an ocean or lake, but he's in just as much danger in the more common bodies of water in a home — open toilets, tubs of water, dishpans of water, and pots of boiling water. Close the lid on your toilet when your cockatiel is in the bathroom with you. Don't let your cockatiel out when pots of water are simmering on the kitchen stove, and keep your eyes peeled for other dangers.

One common, dangerous body of water is a tall glass with interesting liquid in the bottom. Cockatiels are curious, and curiosity about such a drink may tempt them to crawl inside. Unfortunately, they can't crawl back out of a slippery glass. Many cockatiels drown this way, so something as simple as cleaning up your used glasses regularly keeps your cockatiel safe from harm.

Making Time for Play

Your cockatiel treasures the time you spend together socializing and having fun (see Figure 7-1). A young cockatiel's life is all about exploring his environment and playing with other members of his flock. He's just a kid at heart, even though his body is the size of an adult cockatiel. In a flock, he will play by pulling at other cockatiels' long tail feathers. On his own, he will explore every inch of a cage, undo knots on bird toys, and check out any new greens or vegetables you have to offer. Older cockatiels don't lose their curiosity, either, and they enjoy playing with you. Sometimes they're pretty clever about inventing games that involve both of you so that you'll spend more time with them.

Figure 7-1:
Cockatiels love to get out of the cage to play.

Cockatiels can learn many tricks, too. If your cockatiel appears to view learning tricks as play, then go ahead and follow through. Get a good book or videotape on training parrots, and don't let their use of larger birds make you think your cockatiel won't learn the same behaviors. Large parrots are used in shows because they're visible to an audience. Well, you can see your cockatiel on your kitchen table just fine, and you're probably not worried about a career for either of you at a theme park! Learning stimulates a cockatiel's intellect. It also creates a way for interspecies communication to take place, as you reward your cockatiel for doing what you want, when you ask. Once you've both learned one behavior, you'll find that others come quickly. You learn to show your cockatiel to do what you want, and your cockatiel discovers that he can be rewarded for following your directions. Not every cockatiel, however, wants to engage in this kind of structured play. You don't know till you try.

Tricky resources

To learn more about teaching your cockatiel tricks, consult one of these resources:

✔ Tani Robar and Her Fantastic Performing Parrots video series
Robar Productions
3767 S. 194th Street
Seattle, WA 98188
206-878-3010

www.parrottricktraining.com
tani@parrottricktraining.com

✔ The New Parrot Training Handbook by Jennifer Hubbard
1-800-729-7734
www.petbirdxpress.com
info@ birdalog.com

Almost any interaction can be play for your cockatiel. Be open to developing games that either of you start. You can tug-of-war with a string, take turns grooming each other, or form a verbal duet that only the two of you can appreciate. The small size of our cockatiel companions doesn't in any way limit their inventiveness and play.

Playing fetch

Many cockatiels like picking up small toys in their beak and dropping them over the side of their cage. They then run to the edge of the cage and look over the edge, turning their head to get a great look at where their toy has gone. This is the beginning of a game of fetch cockatiel-style. If you retrieve the toy and put it back on top of the cage, chances are good that your cockatiel will pick it back up and drop it over the edge. As you can see, many cockatiels can be trained to do this trick on command — to put items in a receptacle, a basketball in a hoop, or a coin in a bank. In most households, the game stays spontaneous and sporadic and is done just for fun.

Climbing ladders

Ladders can become play toys. You don't have to teach a cockatiel to climb a ladder. If a ladder has rungs at an appropriate spacing, cockatiels will climb it. Cockatiels like to be at the highest vantage point they can reach, and ladders are built to get them there. You can invent games with a ladder. Teach your cockatiel to hold on as you swing it gently down and up again. If he learns to put his wings out and go with the flow, he'll get some needed exercise. If you find a long ladder and lean it against your cockatiel's cage, you can teach your cockatiel to go home on those occasions he flies off his cage.

You teach this behavior by showing your cockatiel what you want. Whenever he flies off his cage, put him on the ladder to get back home. Start out by putting him halfway up the ladder. Eventually, put him at the bottom of the ladder. He'll start getting the idea that he has a way to get home on his own, and eventually he'll find the ladder on his own and march home.

A ladder can also be a convenient perch for a shy cockatiel. If you've acquired an older bird who is shy around hands, or even a young bird who isn't learning the Up command (discussed in Chapter 10) well and seems shy, then teaching him to jump up onto a ladder can be a good way for you to handle that cockatiel. Use the cockatiel's natural wish to get up off the floor when he's off his cage, and say the word "up" when he's getting on a ladder. Repeat the action several times in a row. When your cockatiel knows what is expected of him, he'll practically leap onto a ladder you put out. A ladder closely resembles a perch, which is something familiar to a cockatiel and not nearly as intimidating as a hand or finger.

Getting the bird to come

There's also the "come here" game you can play with your cockatiel. Depending on the rules, you can either train your cockatiel to play this game or he can train you! You can train your cockatiel to come to you, even to fly to you, by associating a command with the action of coming to you. The command can be a word such as "come" or "fly," or it can be a visual command, such as waggling a finger, or a signal, such as snapping your fingers or using a clicker. Start out by using the command when your cockatiel comes to you from close range, similar to the Up command you use to get the bird to land on your finger. Gradually lengthen the distance between the bird and your finger so that he has to travel to get to you. Eventually, your cockatiel will come to you from across the room, either waddling along if he has clipped wings or sailing along if he has a less severe clip or none at all.

It would be great for a cockatiel who accidentally gets outside to know the Come command. One of the reasons lost cockatiels don't get back to their owners is that they don't know how to get down from high places if they happen to be outside. They also have never learned to come. You hope that your cockatiel will never escape, but teaching your cockatiel the Come command and how to come down to you from a high location is good insurance.

In the opposite scenario, your cockatiel can teach you to come when he wants. He is usually subtle about teaching you this, so it's good to be forewarned about how he does it. A single cockatiel who is bonded to you may call out to you. He'll probably call by screaming, though he may also try a whistle. Your cockatiel is meant to live in a flock and to be in touch with flock members constantly. If he knows where you are, your cockatiel will be happy and settle down. In answer to your cockatiel's call, or even before he misses you, you can give him a *contact call* that says, "Here I am, I can hear you" to your cockatiel. This contact call can be those actual words, or it may be a cluck or whistle. It's really less ear-splitting to train your cockatiel to call you softly, say something like "hi," or whistle a certain whistle as a contact call.

Many people come running when their cockatiels call them. The cockatiel picks up on this response pretty fast because seeing you is a reward to him. If you come running, putting on a show and using loud language, all the better. That behavior is a reward to a gregarious bird. If your cockatiel is talented at mimicry, he may start imitating a ringing phone or buzzing microwave when he sees that you come running to those sounds. Using a contact call instead of answering your cockatiel's Come command will keep your household quieter. Reward your cockatiel for sitting and playing quietly and keep him reassured of your presence in the house even when you aren't there interacting directly with him.

Petting a Companion Cockatiel

Your cockatiel will probably appreciate stroking and cuddling, especially if you learn what he likes.

Petting on the head

This may come as a surprise to experienced pet owners, but petting a cockatiel is different from stroking a dog or cat. You pet a dog in the direction of his fur. But your cockatiel likes you to pet him by scratching his head and neck feathers behind his crest in the opposite direction from the way the feathers grow. So when you lift up a cockatiel's feathers just behind his crest, you're petting him in the way he will appreciate most (see Figure 7-2).

Another area where cockatiels like to be petted is just over their ears, also shown in Figure 7-2. Cockatiel ears are not external; they're holes in their heads, just under their bright red cheek patches. They like you to pet that area in a circular, gentle motion. They also like being petted along the ridges of their jowls, along the bottom of their cheekbone. Once you find one of these "sweet spots," your cockatiel will very likely turn his head or put down his head to show you one of the other areas.

Getting your cockatiel to accept other forms of handling

Ideally, while you pet and interact with your cockatiel, you're also training him to accept handling that isn't natural for him to tolerate. For example, without training to tolerate it, a cockatiel won't want to be petted down his back. They're sensitive about handling that would prevent flight or that mimics being held or captured by a predator. Cockatiels, unlike some parrots, don't tolerate being flipped on their back either. They just aren't that kind of parrot; those types of handling aren't in their repertoire of natural positions.

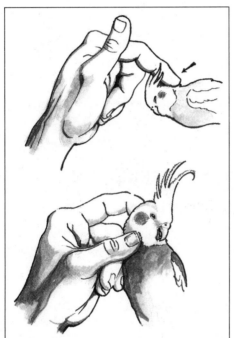

Figure 7-2:
The two best places to pet a cockatiel.

But you have to touch your cockatiel's back during his life. When he sees a veterinarian, you may need to hold and restrain him. You also must restrain your bird to trim his wings and clip his nails (see Chapter 6). Here's what you do to get him used to this form of handling: Occasionally hold your hand lightly over his back (see Figure 7-3). Put more and more pressure on your cockatiel's back, until he readily accepts being restrained without getting frightened. Use this light restraint when you're carrying your cockatiel back to his cage. Then you don't repeatedly have to chase a cockatiel who isn't ready to go back in his cage, or who jumps off your hand for some other reason when you're putting him back in his cage. Keep your hand lightly on his back and keep his head down going in the door. Cockatiels figure out quickly that they can slide off your hand by grabbing the top of the entrance of the cage. Aren't they clever!

Touch your cockatiel's feet sometimes, getting him used to that motion so he isn't so scared if you ever need to look closely at a scratch or bruise on his feet, read his band number, or trim his toenails. Also fan out his wings, supporting his wings by the wing bones. Handle your cockatiel gently and talk to him. Tell him what a beautiful cockatiel he is. When the day comes that you have to clip his wings, he'll be used to the motion and the restraint, and the procedure won't be such a terrifying experience for him.

Figure 7-3:
You can train your cockatiel to accept being touched on his back.

Touching touchy birds

If your cockatiel doesn't like to be touched at all, don't give up. He probably doesn't quite trust you yet or doesn't know how good grooming by his human caretaker can feel. You can slowly win him over. Timing is everything in this game! The next time your resistant cockatiel molts is a good time to get on his good side. Normally, a cockatiel friend helps him groom those itchy pinfeathers that come in where he can't reach. He can't groom his own head, crest, cheeks, and jowls. When you see telltale pinfeathers, introduce him to a light touch by blowing on his head. Try not to scare him. Slowly ruffle the feathers backwards with your breath, and do this briefly when you pass his cage or when he's out of the cage with you.

As your touch-resistant cockatiel gets used to the feel of your breath on his itchy head, introduce a light touch as you blow on him. Do this also when you pass his cage or have him out to play. Gradually work up to using two fingers to "preen" his longest pin feathers on his head and crest. Unpreened pinfeathers are encased in a keratin sheath, which you can roll off between your fingers. New feathers have nerves and blood at their base, so you'll hear about it if you preen too close to your cockatiel's skin! As your cockatiel gets used to your preening, he may solicit it and probably will turn his head so you scratch precisely where it itches.

Photographing Your Cockatiel

One of the fun things you can do with your cockatiel when he's out socializing is to have photo sessions. Photos will become a visual representation of your memories of your cockatiel. A good, clear photo will make a world of difference if your cockatiel is ever lost. On a happier note, you can share photos with your friends and relatives on the Internet. You also can submit photos in contests. Here are some guidelines to achieve better photos of your feathered friend. I can't guarantee that you'll end up with professional photos, but they will be more enjoyable for you and your friends!

- ✔ **Set up your shots.** Your cockatiel may do a lot of cute things in the course of his daily wanderings, but what does the photo background look like? Is the house a mess? A background for a cockatiel can be as simple as a pastel blue posterboard, or a towel pinned to your wall. You can also using an interesting, textured wallpaper, or velvet draped behind your cockatiel. Find a nice perch, convince your cockatiel to sit proudly on it, and snap away.

- ✔ **Keep it simple.** The emphasis should be your cockatiel, not the flower arrangement, a person, or the living room furniture in the picture. Make a photo pertinent to a holiday with colors or a simple accessory. One cockatiel sharing the photo with a whole Christmas tree doesn't work.

- ✔ **Get help from a cockatiel "handler."** Snapping the picture is easier if someone sets up your cockatiel for the picture. Keep your cockatiel's attention. You'll want the handler to get the cockatiel's attention, too. She should whistle, jingle a favorite toy, or call the bird's name. If your cockatiel is getting a little blasé about his modeling career, do something unexpected to perk him up. Lightly pull on a tail feather, or roll a ball or wad of tissues and toss it up or along the floor. Strive for an alert expression in the photo.

- ✔ **Choose a neutral background.** Using a colored background that is neither too dark nor too light works best for most colors of cockatiels. Sky blue seems natural, and many pastel shades work.

- ✔ **Fill up the picture with your cockatiel.** Most people fail to fill enough of the picture with their bird. Although what you see may look good through the camera lens, what you end up with is a cockatiel the size of your thumbnail in the print. Professionals fill the frame with their subject. Make the picture about your cockatiel — and your cockatiel alone.

- ✔ **Use a telephoto or macro lens.** If you have a spiffy camera and can change lenses, use a telephoto lens. Such a lens allows you to be far from your subject but still take a close-up. A macro lens puts you right up at your subject. You'll need to diffuse any flash you use if you're that close. A substitute for a macro lens is a wide-angle lens. A wide-angle lens lets you get close to a subject and still take a photo, but be warned that the image may be slightly distorted.

Eliminate cage bars from your photo. Here's a trick to use when you're taking photos at an aviary or a zoo. Put your lens right up to the cage bars. They won't show up in the picture. If you can't get that close, use the camera's manual controls and focus on the bird in the cage. Otherwise, you may end up with a picture that has the bars of the cage — and not the bird — in focus.

✔ **Soften the flash.** People often take what they think is a great picture of their cockatiel, but the end result is a photo of a cockatiel that's washed out by the flash. Cockatiels are so small that when you're close enough to fill the frame, your flash setting may be too powerful. No matter what kind of camera you have, you can diffuse or soften the flash by putting a tissue over it. Just be sure not to cover the flash light sensor. Experiment with a short roll of film to get the right settings for you and your camera.

✔ **Flash slaves save the day.** A useful little gadget for flash photography is a flash slave sensor. It adds extra light to a scene, helps fill in shadows in backgrounds, and can add a professional halo effect around the head of your bird when placed behind and above the photo subject. You've probably noticed that a studio photographer uses several light sources. You can have a miniature version of that setup, without all the wires. Try using slave sensors, which are triggered by your camera's flash and powered by batteries. You need to experiment to get it right, but using this gadget adds a lot to the shots of your pet.

✔ **Find a way to display or share your photos.** You'll have the most fun taking photos if you can show them off. Start a photo album, make sure that you have a photo for your wallet, and make a key chain, puzzle, mug, or mousepad out of your photos. Be creative. Have fun!

Too Much Freedom: Escaped Cockatiels

Because accidents do happen, someday your cockatiel may fly right out a window or door and become an escaped cockatiel. Of course, preventing that is the best of all possible scenarios. Keep your cockatiel's wings trimmed. Wing feathers grow in about every six months. Even with one feather grown out at the tip of their wings, cockatiels can fly pretty well. Your bird will even develop enough muscle power to sail around to some extent with clipped wings. Trimming wings is covered in Chapter 6.

Most cockatiels don't know what the outside of their houses looks like because that's never been part of their perspective. Consequently, they don't know how to get home. Even if they did know how to get home, cockatiels don't have homing instincts the way pigeons do. In the wild, they are nomadic and don't develop home territories.

Be sure to alert your local animal shelter that your cockatiel is lost. They probably will keep the record and may have posters you can put up. Many community papers also publish "lost pet" ads for free. Describe your bird in simple terms. Not everyone knows what a cockatiel is.

Searching for birdie

A clipped bird won't gain much height once he gets out. Try to find him right away to keep him out of the hands and jaws of neighborhood kids, cats, and hawks. If your cockatiel's wings have entirely grown out, chances are, he'll land in a tree. If you've done any kind of training to get your bird to come or fly to you, or to come down from high places, that effort may pay off. The typical flown-away cockatiel doesn't know how to get down out of a tree, so you need to climb up to his level and calmly ask your cockatiel to step up on your finger and go home.

If you're desperate, wait till dusk, when your cockatiel will find a place to roost, and rescue him then. Drenching the bird with a garden hose so he can't fly is another desperate measure. Using this tactic depends on the proximity of a garden hose, so it's not something you can always do.

Luring him back

If you can't retrieve your cockatiel but he's still in the area, leave his cage out. Eventually he'll be hungry enough to look for food, and the familiar environment and the food will look good. Just in case your cockatiel is the friendly sort who would go to a stranger, be sure to look in the "found" ads of your local paper.

Familiar things, such as his cage and favorite treats, will draw your cockatiel back to your house. If at all possible, make a recording of your cockatiel's contact call to keep on hand for such an emergency. If you can borrow a second cockatiel or use one of your own, take that bird outside in a secure cage and let him call to the escaped bird. Whistle your cockatiel's favorite tune or use his contact call. Follow your bird as long as you have him in your field of vision. At the very least, you want to know in what direction he headed. You can pinpoint his location if he calls to another cockatiel or answers your contact calls.

Getting help

Alert anyone who may know where your cockatiel is or who is likely to hear about a found cockatiel. These people include your avian veterinarian, local pet stores, feed stores, animal shelters, bird clubs, bird groomers, and bird boarders. Put up posters in the vicinity where your cockatiel was lost and place a "lost" ad in the paper. Birds can travel quite far, so don't be surprised if you get a call eventually from someone who lives three to ten miles from you and who has found your bird.

Be prepared to identify your cockatiel if someone claims to have found him. Many people assume that a bird on the loose belongs to whomever finds him, or that someone negligent enough to let a bird go doesn't deserve to have him back. Understand that these are common feelings among the general public, even though you know how much you love your cockatiel and want him back. To identify your cockatiel, who may not look as handsome or well kept as the bird who left your care, know his band number or bring along a photo that shows an identifying mark on your cockatiel. If he has special markings or is missing toes, those are helpful ID marks.

If you start to lose hope or need help finding your cockatiel, you may want to contact people who find lost birds as a business. These people may provide bird care, pet sitting, or behavioral consultation as a business and also offer this service. Animal communicators, or those who talk telepathically to animals, also have some success finding lost birds. Look for one in the phone book, ask at bird stores, or search on the Internet for "animal communicator." Your best chance of finding your cockatiel is to get the word out in the network of people in your community who work with and enjoy companion birds. Then you'll have several sets of ears and eyes on the lookout, including the Internet community. You may post lost bird listings to mailing lists and Web sites. Some places to post listings of lost birds include the following:

- ✔ www.birdhotline.com
- ✔ http://birdmart.com
- ✔ http://birdsnways.com/birds/blost.htm
- ✔ http://forum.unclescrotor.com
- ✔ www.counsel.net/pets/prs/lostfound.html
- ✔ www.mickaboo.org/doyou.htm

Chapter 8

Vacationing with or without Your Cockatiel

. . . .

. . . .

During the first few weeks of cockatiel ownership — while you're still in the blush of discovery and first love for your cockatiel — you may think you'll never leave your cockatiel. The time will come, however, when you want to visit family or business takes you out of town. But you may not have to leave your cockatiel; many people travel with their pet birds. Be a good bird owner if you travel. Doing so ensures that your relatives will welcome you back (and may not be able resist getting their own cockatiel before long) and that hotels will continue to welcome pets. You also have plenty of opportunities as you travel to become ambassadors for good bird care and cockatiel ownership. You'll meet a lot of people while traveling with your cockatiel: those who have birds of their own and those who are curious about your feathered companion.

If you can't take your cockatiel on this trip, then you have some other choices to make. Should you board your cockatiel at a facility? Should you rely on friends to care for your cockatiel? Should you hire a pet sitter in your community? Of course you want to leave your cockatiel in competent hands, with a caretaker who understands birds, their needs, and the care they require. You want to have a good time while you're on vacation and know that your cockatiel is well cared for. The information in this chapter can help.

Deciding Whether to Take or Leave Your Cockatiel

You may have no choice about taking or leaving your cockatiel. If you're going to be traveling by bus or train, for example, your cockatiel will not be welcome along for the ride. Absolutely no animals can be taken as passengers or sent as baggage or cargo on passenger buses, cruise ships, or trains. That restriction leaves cars and planes as available means of transportation if you're traveling with your bird. Yes, Columbus took New World parrots back to the Old World on his ships, but the rules and regulations have changed since then.

In some situations, the best decision is to leave your cockatiel at home. If you're visiting someone who's allergic to birds, it's most polite to abide by the rules of the house and to consider the health of the household members. If you're traveling on business, caring for a cockatiel is a low priority compared to increasing business and networking with business associates. Some birds get carsick, and you don't need to inflict that torment on your companion.

Cockatiels love routine as much as we do and thrive in their home environment. That's another argument against taking your cockatiel with you. If you have your cockatiel cared for at home, she'll be most comfortable and most at ease during your trip. She may miss you, but at least her environment will be familiar. She can live in her own cage and be in her own home, where she knows the sounds of your home and its indoor as well as outdoor environment.

Just as a vacation, especially to an exotic place, can help you learn to adapt to a new setting, boarding your cockatiel can help her become more "familiar" with and comfortable in a new environment. Leave her with a pet sitter for a day or two when you aren't traveling. Get feedback from the pet sitter, and coach her about how to make your cockatiel feel at home. You'll probably find that you have habits you haven't told a pet sitter about. There's the 1-inch square of dry toast your cockatiel gets in the morning, or the time at which you cover her cage in the evening. You can also explain to a pet sitter what words or commands your bird understands. A trial run can help your cockatiel feel at home in more than one location and give you a chance to answer your pet sitter's questions.

Finding a Caretaker

Beyond a doubt, you want your cockatiel to have the best care possible when you aren't with her. As you have been discovering by reading this book and caring for your own cockatiel, a companion bird has special needs. Birds are a special kind of pet, and cockatiels are a special kind of bird. The caretaker of your companion should know something about birds or be willing to learn.

As you consider whether to travel with your cockatiel or to leave her in the care of another person, consider the qualifications of a potential caregiver. Friends and family may offer free care, but if they're scared of your bird, how well will your cockatiel be cared for? You may be more comfortable dealing with a professional, such as a professional pet sitter. If all of a sitter's clients are dogs and cats, however, even a professional needs to be willing to learn about bird care requirements.

Make sure that the pet sitter meets your standard for providing quality care in your absence. Will your caregiver expose your cockatiel to predatory animals such as dogs and cats? Will your small cockatiel be in a safe place? A facility or a home in which your cockatiels are exposed to the prying eyes of a predatory animal could mean that is a very stressful place to send your cockatiel, unless your bird and the animal are friends. Does your caregiver understand that birds are susceptible to fumes and chemicals? Any facility that also uses flea dips or does grooming may not be acceptable lodging for a cockatiel.

How about a friend?

It's as important for your cockatiel to have her own friends as it is for you. Your cockatiel will choose her own friends, just as you choose yours. A cockatiel's special friend among your acquaintances is a potential caretaker when you're out of town. Your cockatiel's friend may also be approached as being named as a more permanent caretaker in case anything happens to you. You can see how important it is to recognize the special people in your cockatiel's life and to make sure that she has some human friends.

A cockatiel's human friends may jump at the chance to care for your cockatiel while you're away. Give them proper training. Caring for a cockatiel full-time is different from fawning over one for an hour or two while visiting your home. Be sure to firm up the arrangements so that there aren't any resentments. Do you need to pay your friend a pet-sitting fee, or does the friend consider this an opportunity to play with your cockatiel, with no other reimbursement needed? You may be able to trade pet sitting services with your friend, so that you care for her dog the next time she's out of town or you plant her flower garden next spring. What are friends for? Just be sure to firm up these arrangements by actually talking about compensation in advance.

Provide enough food to last the time you are gone, and leave money for your friend to replenish fresh veggies if you're taking an extended trip. Let your avian veterinarian know that you're out of town and your friend has your permission to bring her in if necessary. Or leave a letter with that information your friend can use.

There's nothing like an accident to cool a friendship. Be aware that things happen, so don't hold your pet sitter responsible for the loss or death of your cockatiel due to an accident while the bird is in his or her care. Talk about this aspect of caring for your cockatiel. Expect your friend to make her best effort to keep your bird from harm.

Try a pet sitter

Professional pet sitters often advertise in local papers or post notices at veterinary offices, pet shops, or feed stores. Most pet sitters earn their bread and butter, or kibble and gravy as it were, from dog and cat clients. You may have to phone a few pet sitters before you find one who knows how to care for a cockatiel. For more ideas about pet sitters, two professional pet-sitting organizations in the United States have toll-free referral phone numbers:

- ✔ National Association of Professional Pet Sitters (NAPPS): 1200 G Street, NW, Suite 760, Washington, DC 20005; referrals 1-800-296-PETS, phone 202-393-3317, fax 202-393-0336; Web site www.petsitters.org

- ✔ Pet Sitters International (PSI): Pet Sitters International, 418 East King St., King, NC 27021. referrals 800-268-7487; phone 336-983-9222; Web site www.petsit.com

After you've located a couple potential pet sitters, they will ask for an interview with you and your cockatiel to see how the sitters get along with your bird. Make sure that you're comfortable with this person who will have a key to your house and who receives premium rates for her work. Observe the interaction between your cockatiel and your potential pet sitter. Show your pet sitter where you keep the daily supplies and any stockpiled necessities. Explain whether you freeze bird treats or have a dispenser for bottled or filtered water. Ask your pet sitter about birds she owns or cares for and share your knowledge of cockatiels. Discuss whether you want your cockatiel out of the cage while your pet sitter is caring for her. Let the sitter know whether you use a special word or action to coax your cockatiel back into her cage. Is there a special bribe the pet sitter can use if the need arises?

A pet sitter can make a home look lived-in, creating a deterrent to thieves or mischief makers. Talk to your pet sitter about bringing in the mail and a daily newspaper, turning on lights in different parts of the house, and opening and closing blinds. If you have plants, ask the sitter to water them. Many pet sitters request a check when you leave, and others settle up upon your return.

On your part, it's polite to call your pet sitter when you're back home. A sitter may worry about the pets under her care at the end of an assignment if she isn't sure that their owner is home safe.

Picking up germs

Tremendous advances have been made in avian medicine over the last two decades. We can test for or vaccinate against many avian diseases that are incurable. Not everyone takes advantage of these advances, however. The deadliest diseases are passed on through the air or through droppings, not necessarily by contact with an infected bird. Any location that has a number of birds but doesn't have strict rules of cleanliness puts your bird at risk. Cockatiels themselves do well if they have *psittacosis,* a disease for which there is still not a definitive test, though it is treatable. If your cockatiel is carrying psittacosis, however, she may make other birds sick, or may catch it from another cockatiel who hasn't yet been diagnosed with the disease.

A healthy cockatiel successfully wards off illness, even if exposed to it. You should question whether you should take a chance boarding a bird in a facility where she will be exposed to other birds. What precautions does the boarding facility take? Is your cockatiel at risk? If the facility requires a recent health check by an avian veterinarian, that is a step in the right direction. Does the facility provide clean cages and fresh vegetables for its boarders? Does it have standards of cleanliness that prevent the transmission of disease from one bird to another? Look for good air quality in the facility, attendants who wash their hands in between handling different birds, and birds who are kept in separate rooms.

One of the most bird germ-laden places in your community is the office of your avian veterinarian. It is also staffed by some of the most skilled people regarding bird care and minimizing the transmission of infection. Consider those aspects of boarding your bird with a veterinarian if that is one of your options.

Boarding a Cockatiel

If you have to leave your cockatiel behind while traveling, you'd ideally like to keep her at home where a familiar and friendly caretaker can watch her. But sometimes you may have to take your cockatiel to a boarding facility.

Facilities that sometimes board birds include veterinary hospitals, kennels, pet stores, and actual bird boarding facilities. Sometimes pet sitters take animals into their homes. Any facility that boards a number of animals is interested in maintaining the health of its visitors. To board a cockatiel at a professional facility, you will probably be asked to supply records of a current veterinary exam. If you don't need to provide one, then neither do other birds boarded. Don't use that facility. Dogs and cats who are boarded have been inoculated against major diseases. Vaccines haven't yet been developed for most bird diseases, however, so you need to be careful about contact with birds of an unknown health status. Try to choose a facility whose staff is knowledgeable about birds. Such a place will be most likely to handle your cockatiel properly and be most willing to meet her needs while you're out of town.

Familiar is better

Your cockatiel will handle the stress of being away from home if you leave her with familiar, cockatiel-friendly people. If she doesn't know her caretaker, leave here there a couple afternoons to familiarize her with the people and surroundings. You'll find out her response to being left, and her caretakers will find out how they like living with your cockatiel. If you do this for short trial periods, then you can discuss your bird's behavior and answer the caretaker's questions before you take off on your trip.

Write a book

There's no such thing as providing too much information for your boarding facility or pet sitter. This is your chance to be an author. Prepare a book of information for the pet caretaker. For starters, let your surrogate cockatiel parent know where you can be reached. If you have an itinerary, give lodging information for each day of your trip. In this age of cell phones, maybe that's all the communication you need to worry about. If you plan to call in to your answering machine or to voice mail or check e-mail, include that contact information.

List your cockatiel's name and description. If you have several birds, your pet's caretaker will want to call them by name.

If there's an emergency while you're gone, you want your pet's caretaker to know where to get veterinary care. List phone numbers for your avian veterinarian and for an emergency clinic that is open late and on the weekend. If you don't know the latter, ask your veterinarian to refer you to one. Inform your veterinarian that you'll be gone, or leave a signed statement authorizing your caretaker to provide veterinary care in your absence. If you have a dollar limit on the amount of care your veterinarian can provide or any other considerations, put that information in black and white.

What your pet's caretaker wants to know most about your cockatiel is her feeding schedule and her daily routine. Describe the care that should be provided, including offering food and fresh water every day, serving vegetables, and covering the cage overnight. None of these tasks are as simple as they sound. You do a lot of things automatically that other people may not think of, so be sure to provide specific information. For example, specify whether you serve your cockatiel bottled water or tap water. Explain that the water dish should be washed with soap and water before being refilled to prevent a slime buildup in the bowls. If you provide clean water whenever it is soiled, be sure to mention that, too.

When describing your cockatiel's main diet, be specific. Mention that you dump out old food after a day and you fill only the bottom of the bowl. To make the job easier, draw a line on the side of the bowl with the words "Fill to here." Require the person boarding your pet to use the designated scoop to get clean food from the main supply. Be sure to explain that your cockatiel will make dust of her pellets or that seed hulls need to be blown from the top of her dish.

Let your cockatiel caretaker know that creativity is allowed when serving vegetables. Explain that you thread parsley through the cage bars, chop vegetables finely, or microwave them. If you take dishes of fresh food out of the cage after a certain length of time, specify that. Don't assume that your caretaker has read this book or knows anything about *your* routine, even if she also keeps birds.

Make a list of other people who know your cockatiel to use as a resource if the caretaker has a question. These people may be family, friends, a neighbor, a teenage visitor, or members of a bird club who can answer technical questions about birds.

The fun part is sharing your cockatiel. If your cockatiel loves specific toys, dances to a certain song or artist, or says certain words, detail that for the caretaker. If you say words that are meaningful to your cockatiel, be sure that the caretaker knows about them. For example, do you say "night night" before covering the cage, "hello" when you come in from outside, or "time to go back," when play time outside the cage is over? Sharing these tips can make your cockatiel's boarding experience fun for everyone concerned!

Taking Your Bird on a Road Trip

You and your bird can safely travel by car with the proper preparations. Necessary extras for traveling with birds include the following:

- Bird first-aid kit
- Supply of towels
- Light-colored or white sheet
- Spray bottle
- Familiar toys
- Supply of food and veggies
- Water from home
- Travel cage or carrier

A cockatiel can thoroughly enjoy car rides. Your cockatiel may watch the scenery or chirp excitedly when you're off on a trip. If your bird is unsettled by the car ride, putting a light sheet over her cage may make her more secure while still providing light. Lowering the noise level may calm a frightened or raucous cockatiel. Turn down the radio and speak softly. Model the behavior you want from your cockatiel instead of yelling and adding to the fracas. Our first reaction is often to do something that will only stimulate a bird to make more noise. Finally, you may want to do a few test drives before heading out on a long trip with your birds. A very few birds get carsick. In that case, providing in-home care or boarding the bird is the best thing to do.

In cold weather, wrap a bird's carrier or cage in towels when transporting her between the heated environment of a building and a car. In warm weather, use a spray bottle filled with water to cool off a bird. Spraying a warm bird under the wings and on the feet cools her off the fastest. In the summer, always travel with a water spray bottle, as temperatures vary in different regions and throughout the day.

To know how your bird is doing on a trip, be aware that cold birds shiver and warm birds pant and hold their wings out away from their body. The best advice is to avoid extremes of temperatures, but you still need to know what to do in case of emergency.

Do not leave your pets in an automobile. Cars heat up quickly, and excessive heat is deadly.

Travel cage

Depending on the size of your cockatiel's cage, you may have to make special arrangements when traveling by car. Strap your cockatiel's cage into the car with a seat belt, and use a cage that easily fits in the car. Many cockatiels can travel in their own cages by car, with some modifications (see Figure 8-1). Take out the toys before a trip and substitute greens for water. Birds who live in a larger enclosure can travel happily in a smaller size cage or a carrier. All cages should be equipped with some kind of perch so that your bird doesn't have to travel flat-footed for the entire trip.

If your bird will be traveling in a carrier, think about overnight accommodations. Many types of fold-down travel cages are available, or you could get a small cage at your destination that will be adequate for a short time. Smaller cages come in handy when traveling, when a bird is boarded, and for trips to the avian veterinarian. When you stop for rest or a meal, offer your cockatiel fresh water and a treat.

Figure 8-1:
You should remove toys and the water dish from the travel cage, but keep the perch.

State laws

If you're crossing state borders within the United States, look up laws and regulations that pertain to the importation of exotic birds in that state. You may be able to obtain that information from your avian veterinarian. If not, it is available from the United States Department of Agriculture, Animal and Plant Health Inspection Service (APHIS), which has a veterinarian in each state. You can contact the USDA-APHIS-VS at 4700 River Road, Riverdale, MD 20737; phone 301-734-5097; Web site www.aphis.usda.gov.

Laws and regulations about exotic birds vary from state to state. Some states regulate sales, others oversee ownership, and some only specify certain species that are not allowed, such as Quaker parakeets or Patagonian conures. Cockatiels may be kept in every state, but some states may have laws governing how you may purchase one and whether the bird needs to be banded.

State laws and regulations are constantly changing. To be sure of current laws, contact the conservation or wildlife office of the state to which you are traveling or driving through with your birds before scheduling the trip. Some states have regulations about banding birds or registering them. Laws and regulations regarding exotic birds are usually overseen by the conservation or wildlife division of each state's government. To find out more, contact that specific department in each state. Your avian veterinarian may also be able to help you identify the governing body involved and the current state laws regarding companion birds.

Accommodations

If your trip will be overnight or last several days, one challenge is finding accommodations that will accept both you and your bird or birds. Inquire at each motel to check regulations there, or check the motel directory. Books and handbooks on traveling with pets often list this type of information. These are generally oriented to the dog owner, but most accommodations that accept pet dogs also accept birds, so they're a good resource. You can find such a guide at your local library, at bookstores, or on the Web.

Books about traveling with your pet are available from these sources:

Millennium Publishing Group
1271 Tenth Street, Suite D
Monterey, CA 93940
800-524-6826
sales@millpub.com
www.millpub.com/pw-se.shtml

Gene R. Sower
8 Windsor Place
Montclair, NJ 07043
genesis104@aol.com
www.lucy-the-dog.com

Dawbert Press, Inc.
P.O. Box 2758
Duxbury, MA 02331
800-93-DAWBERT
dawbert@thecia.net
www.gorp.com/dawbert/

Here are some suggested Web sites that deal with traveling with a pet:

- www.petswelcome.com
- http://takeyourpet.com
- www.petfriendlytravel.com

When you're traveling, keep in mind that Motel 6 usually accepts pets (1-800-4MOTEL6).

Because cockatiel owners want to continue to be welcome at pet-friendly inns, take care of the room and your own birds when staying there. For example, put towels down on dressers or tables before setting a bird cage on it. Carry a sheet or plastic to spread around the cage if your bird flings food.

Though you may be welcome guests, it is not a good idea to leave your birds unattended in a motel room. If your bird damages anything, talk to the manager about it and offer to pay for the damage. Finally, don't forget your bird when you leave!

 Did you know that your bird could stay at Disneyland or Disney World while you enjoy the sights? These theme parks, as well as others, have on-site kennels to accommodate their visitors who travel with pets. It's worth looking into if you're going to visit such an attraction as part of your trip.

Flying with Your Bird

When planning to fly with a bird (in an airplane anyway), advance planning is a good idea. Call ahead to get reservations for both yourself and your bird. Some airlines don't allow pets to travel in the passenger compartments of their planes, and others have a limit on the number of pets who can travel on the plane or within each class of seating. You can also find out how many birds are allowed on the plane with you, if that's an issue. Often, two or more smaller birds can travel with you if they fit in one carrier. Your crate or travel carrier must fit under a seat in the airplane. If you don't know where else to get an appropriate carrier, the airlines themselves often sell them. Ask the airline reservation assistant about this. Airlines charge a fee for your bird if she travels as carry-on baggage or rides in either the baggage or cargo compartments. Ask about the fee. Often, that fee is paid at the ticket counter when you show up with your ticket and with your bird or birds in a carrier. If you're making a round trip, you pay a fee each way. Most airlines require that a bird traveling with them also have a valid health certificate from a veterinarian within ten days of flying. Arrangements do vary by airline, so talk to a reservations agent well before your scheduled flight.

Make your companion comfortable for the flight. Make sure that your cockatiel bird has firm footing in his carrier by lining it with artificial grass, pine bedding, or a towel. Also provide some kind of perch for your cockatiel, situated very low in the carrier. Provide a dry feed and some juicy foods, like lettuce or parsley. These greens replace water, which would slosh all over during the trip. Don't put toys in the carrier because they can become dangerous projectiles when traveling. Take along a towel to cover your bird if things get too stimulating. Airline carriers have ventilation holes on all sides, so your bird will probably peek out at you through these. You may want to pack some water from home for the transition time when you arrive at your destination. It will be less stressful for your bird to drink the water she is used to receiving, rather than make one more adjustment in a new environment.

International Travel

For birds, international travel is usually by air. Depending on your trip, you probably need to plan far ahead. Procedures and guidelines are in place if you're planning to take a bird on vacation with you overseas, to move overseas, to bring a pet bird back home from overseas if you have lived outside the country for at least a year, or to engage in international trade by selling or buying a bird internationally. Some bird species are endangered, and import into the U.S. of most bird species is restricted. Traveling with a bird into and out of the U.S. requires certain fees, permits, and procedures. Permits required may take from five weeks to several months to obtain. For international travel, contact the U.S. Fish and Wildlife Service, Office of Management Authority, regarding CITES (Convention on International Trade in Endangered Species) export and/or import permits, the USDA regarding quarantine, the airline on which you or the bird are traveling, and the proper authorities in the country where your bird is going or from which it is coming. Here is some contact information that you might find helpful:

- U.S. Fish and Wildlife Service, Office of Management Authority, 4401 N. Fairfax Dr., Room 700, Arlington, VA 22203; phone 800-358-2104; fax: 703-358-2281.

- U.S. Department of Agriculture, Animal and Plant Health Inspection Service (APHIS), phone 800-245-6340; Web site www.aphis.usda.gov. For information on foreign requirements on animal export, call the USDA at 301-734-8383 or visit its Web site at www.aphis.usda.gov/vs/ireg_txt/.

Pamphlets and flyers are available from both of the U.S. Fish and Wildlife Service and the U.S. Department of Agriculture to help you understand the procedures required to travel with or ship a bird between countries. Some parrots are endangered species, so arrangements are even more complex.

Pets traveling round trip

Pets traveling with you when you are abroad may be exempted from the USDA quarantine and foreign certification requirements. The exception applies only to birds of U.S. origin and only if you make special arrangements in advance. You still must obtain all relevant USDA and USFWS documents before leaving the United States. Contact U.S. Fish and Wildlife to obtain a CITES export permit, which allows you to bring your pet bird back into the United States without a separate import permit. Be sure to validate the permit with U.S. Fish and Wildlife Service at time of export and keep a copy. Call U.S. Fish and Wildlife, Office of Management Authority, to get an application for a CITES permit (Form 3-200).

You must also obtain any permits you need to comply with the Wild Bird Conservation Act. While overseas, you must keep your pet bird separate from other birds and then arrange to have it inspected by a USDA-APHIS veterinarian, for a fee, when you return to the United States. Your bird must come through one of the ports of entry approved for birds or any airport that can be serviced by a USDA veterinary official. For more information, contact USDA-APHIS-VS at 4700 River Road, Riverdale, MD 20737; 301-734-5097.

If you don't want to wade through the forms and procedures alone, consider hiring a private company or a U.S. customs broker to take care of much of the logistics of traveling with or shipping a bird internationally. The Independent Pet and Animal Transportation Association recommends that you look up "pet transportation" in the Yellow Pages. A pet transporter can take care of everything involved in moving or shipping a bird, including permits required. These services come with a fee, of course.

Travel to Canada

Pets coming from Canada to the U.S. are exempt from quarantine but must be inspected by a USDA-APHIS veterinarian. A fee is charged for this inspection, and you must make arrangements in advance whether you're driving into the United States or the cockatiel is being shipped into the United States by air. If coming into the United States from Canada by automobile, you must arrange for a veterinary inspection at a USDA-designated land border station. You must provide the APHIS veterinarian at the station with a signed statement that certifies your bird has been in your possession for at least 90 days, is healthy, and has been kept separate from other birds. For information about ports of entry, contact USDA-APHIS-VS at 4700 River Road, Riverdale, MD 20737; 301-734-5097.

Purchasing a bird overseas

You can buy a cockatiel overseas and bring it home as your pet, though there are certain conditions to this arrangement. For example, an individual can import only two pet birds and must have resided outside of the United States for at least one year. Do get necessary permits before shipping the bird to the United States, and arrange for quarantine. Permits required include the following:

- ✔ Health certificate from exporting country within 30 days of shipment to U.S. (Provide a translation if the certificate is not in English.) VS Form 17-23 includes an acceptable health certificate in English.
- ✔ Wild Bird Conservation Act (WBCA) permit to import a bird acquired outside the U.S.

Also obtain a CITES export permit form the bird's country of origin (if appropriate).

To reserve quarantine space at a USDA animal import facility, write to the USDA port veterinarian at the port of entry and request Veterinary Services (VS) Form 17-23. You pay when making reservations. A charge is associated with quarantine. Pet birds must enter the United States through one of these U.S. quarantine stations:

- **Honolulu, Hawaii:** Port Veterinarian, 3375 Koapaka St., Suite H420, Honolulu, HI 96819; phone 808-861-8560; fax 808-861-8570

- **Los Angeles, California:** Port Veterinarian, 9680 S. La Cienega Blvd., Inglewood, CA 90301; phone 310-215-2352; fax 310-215-1314

- **McAllen, Texas:** Port Veterinarian, 320 N. Main St.; Room 135, McAllen, TX 78501; phone 210-687-8314; fax 210-687-1267

- **Miami, Florida:** Port Veterinarian, P.O. Box 660657, Miami Springs, FL 33266; phone 305-526-2926; fax 305-526-2929

- **New York, New York:** Port Veterinarian, JFK International Airport, Cargo Building 77, Room 116, Jamaica, NY 11430; phone 718-553-1727; fax 718-553-7543

- **San Ysidro, California:** Port Veterinarian, P.O. Box 126, San Ysidro, CA 92073; phone 310-215-2352; fax 310-215-1314

Part III
Behavior and Training

The 5th Wave By Rich Tennant

"I really don't think there's anything funny about teaching the cockatiel to sing the theme song from 'Mission Impossible' everytime I use my Ab-Cruncher."

In this part . . .

I explain in detail the normal behaviors that you're likely to see in your cockatiel, and I cover some basic training principles. I also show you what to do when your cockatiel misbehaves.

Chapter 9

Understanding Normal Cockatiel Behaviors

*T*o know a cockatiel is to love one. They have winning dispositions and fit into many kinds of modern-day families. They're patient with working people, gentle with children, company for the elderly, study buddies for students of all ages, and members of bustling families as they chime right in to the din around them. As much as you love your cockatiel, though, you may wonder about some of his habits. If this is the only cockatiel you know, you want to know whether you have one who is normal or a freak, right? If this is your only bird companion, you'll notice that his behavior is very different from a dog's or cat's behavior.

You yell "come" for example, and a dog comes running — or it does after a little obedience training. Your cockatiel imitates the phone or the microwave, and you come running. What's different about the relationship you have with these two companion animals? A dog and maybe a cat will fetch a ball when you throw it; a cockatiel will throw a ball or toy off his cage repeatedly if *you* fetch it for him! This is a topsy-turvy world for the new bird owner. A bird is a really different kind of pet. Their sharp senses are their ears and eyes. Though cockatiels living in our homes are many generations removed from the wild, they developed instincts of a prey animal. Because we're used to predator companions in our canine and feline friends, some cockatiel behaviors may seem odd and are certainly different.

Even if you've had other birds, a cockatiel may have behaviors you wonder about! We keep hundreds of species of birds in captivity. Each is adapted to a different environment in the wild, and many represent the first generation or two in captivity in the United States. Cockatiels have been kept as pets in Western civilization for 150 years. By contrast, dogs and cats are species in which different breeds have been developed. Generations and generations of dogs have resided with and been helpmates to humans for the past 15,000 years. Cats have resided with or near humans since the time of the Egyptian pharaohs. The only bird species in which we see breeds is the canary, domesticated for the past 500 years. This all means that cockatiels don't necessarily have a lot in common with our other species of companion birds. Some of their behaviors differ drastically from the behavior of other common bird species. Lovebirds are native to Africa and build nests, for example. Conures are native to South and Central American grasslands and rain forests. Cockatiels are native to the Australian desert. Survival skills in these habitats vary a lot and affect the behavior of our cockatiel companions.

Is Your Cockatiel Being Weird?

After you've had your cockatiel for two weeks to six months, you will have seen many of his behaviors, and you may wonder about some of them. Below is a list of many of the behavior issues that come up for new cockatiel owners. Ask your bird breeder, pet store, or avian veterinarian about behavior that you feel may indicate a health concern or a behavior problem. For your own peace of mind, the following sections explain normal behaviors.

Preening

Cockatiels seem to spend one-third of their life preening. This is the activity you see your cockatiel engaging in when he runs his feathers through his beak. What he's doing is taking oil from a gland at the base of his tail and applying it to each feather. A cockatiel is very thorough about this. He'll preen each feather on his chest and back, each feather in his wings, and each tail feather as well, bending it to reach the very tip. He'll also spend some time cleaning his feet and may rub his beak on a perch for the final touch. You'll see the payoff when you shower your cockatiel and notice that the water beads up on his back That means he's taking excellent care of his feathers, and in turn he's well prepared for being rained on and for dealing naturally with temperature changes. So what if there aren't a lot of thunderstorms or cold fronts at your house? Your desert-adapted cockatiel is still prepared, conditioned by centuries of adapting to wild conditions before joining you in your living room.

A cockatiel's feathers are very important to his well being. When he's hot, he slicks them down. When he's chilly, he fluffs up his feathers to make himself a down comforter for warmth. A film of oil on his feathers helps him repel water so he doesn't get wet and chilled.

Cockatiels preen for another reason: to zip up any feathers that have been ruffled. Zip, I said. Yes, zip. Cockatiel feathers are made up of many strands that connect to the central shaft of a feather. Each strand is covered with *barbules* that keep a feather looking like one piece by connecting with each other, something like hook-and-loop closures. You can see this if you run your finger over a loose feather that is disconnected in a place or two. Whoosh, and the feather is back in one piece again, good as new. So much to do, so little time, if you're a cockatiel. You have to keep your feathers well oiled and arranged nicely, keep the dust to a minimum, and make sure that every feather is zipped up so that it efficiently does its job of holding in heat and being beautiful.

Scratching

Cockatiels don't get fleas, but they do spend time scratching. This is part of their preening behavior, which a cockatiel uses to keep its feathers in top condition. Much of the time, cockatiels scratch their head feathers. In a flock, they may ask another cockatiel to preen their head feathers, but single cockatiels learn to use their feet to scratch where it itches. Cockatiels are quite acrobatic scratchers. They quite improbably lift their leg up over their wing in order to scratch their head.

You can keep scratching to a minimum by giving your cockatiel frequent baths. Doing so keeps the skin moist and healthy and encourages cockatiels to preen their feathers. Use tepid water coming from a plant sprayer or mister, or encourage your cockatiel to sit in a steamy bathroom while you shower.

Dusting your house

Somehow companion birds and cleaning up go together. That's one of the commitments you make when taking on bird ownership. Cockatiels offer a real challenge in this department, as they have down feathers that disintegrate into dust. You can see the dust and fluff float into the air when a cockatiel is sunbathing or sitting in a strong light. The cockatiel's bigger cousins, the cockatoos, have even more and bigger down feathers, so that if you snuggle with one, you're likely to end up with white powder on your hands or face. For a small bird, a cockatiel can generate a lot of dust, and of course, more cockatiels generate more dust. You'll be happiest living with several cockatiels if you invest in an air cleaner or purifier of some kind to run near cockatiel cages. You can keep cockatiel dust to a minimum by spraying your feathered companion often with water from a plant sprayer. Doing so encourages her to preen her feathers.

Dandruff

Many new cockatiel owners worry about the flakes of "dandruff" that appear on a cockatiel from time to time. If you understand how a cockatiel grows new feathers, this won't be a mysterious occurrence at all. New feathers, which normally come in twice a year, or more often in some well-heated homes, have a plastic-looking keratin sheath. This sheath falls away in flakes as a feather matures. It may look like dandruff, but it's nothing of the sort.

If your cockatiel scratches incessantly or scratches as though he has an itch, it's time to schedule a trip to your avian veterinarian. A bird vet can do tests to determine whether parasites or a skin infection may be causing excessive scratching.

Rousing and tail waggles

Rousing is a term used by falconers that describes the all-over rustle a raptor does when he changes from one activity to another. I borrowed the term for this book because cockatiels have a similar behavior that signifies "Okay, on to the next order of business." When a cockatiel has finished preening or eating, or preening a companion, he fluffs out all his feathers, shakes his body from head to toe, and finishes by waggling his tail. Then he'll change activities, or he may not go on to anything special besides sitting or napping.

A little waggle of the tail at the end of a total body shake is normal. If a cockatiel is pumping his tail up and down repeatedly, then he's having trouble breathing. Schedule an appointment with your avian veterinarian if you see tail-pumping behavior.

Yawning

Cockatiels occasionally open their mouth and yawn repeatedly. Bird people call this *gaping*, and it's a normal cockatiel behavior, if it happens on occasion. This action may cause you concern, however. You may wonder whether a seed is stuck in your cockatiel's throat or whether he's having trouble swallowing, or whether you can do something to help. Most gaping is normal and signals boredom the way a human yawn does. It may be an action that allows a cockatiel to adjust his *crop,* which is a part of a cockatiel's digestive system that humans don't have. You don't know what it would be like to send your dinner to a crop first, before it went on to be digested.

Though occasional yawns are normal for a cockatiel, repeated gaping could signal a bacterial or a yeast infection. Your avian veterinarian knows how to test for and treat either type of infection.

Extending wings

You know that you can tell a great deal about how your cockatiel is feeling by the way his crest is positioned. More rarely, a cockatiel may use wing displays to communicate with you or another bird. The most extreme gesture your cockatiel can make is to extend his wings to their full length and then to hold them up over his head for several seconds. A cockatiel will repeat this motion several times if he thinks he needs to do so for someone else to get the message. A cockatiel will look as big as he can possibly get with this posture.

When a cockatiel holds his wings high up over his head, that means he is staking out his territory, saying "this is mine," or showing another cockatiel "I'm top bird around here." A cockatiel may use this signal to claim territory or a mate. He also may use it when another cockatiel is seen as a threat. When two cockatiels, usually males, encounter each other and you see this display from one of them, he's trying to convince the other he's in control, top dog, at the top of the heap, leader, and highest in the pecking order. Rarely, a cockatiel may put on this display if he's claiming his cage or aviary when an unfamiliar human being is about.

Cockatiel squabbles most often consist of posturing and vocalization. Two cockatiels who aren't getting along are likely to peck at each other's feet, wrestle beaks while chattering, and lift their wings over their heads.

Flapping in place

Cockatiels hang upside down for short periods of time, with their wings extended, to show that a nest site is theirs. Pet birds do this from curtain rods or from a perch, lampshade, or other spot where they feel comfortable in your house. The message is "This is mine, life is wonderful." It's unusual behavior, but you shouldn't be concerned. Your cockatiel hasn't suddenly been bitten by a vampire or taken up batty ways.

If your cockatiel flaps vigorously while holding on to a perch, he is exercising. He instinctively knows that his wing muscles are for flying far and fast. Chances are, he doesn't get much of a chance to do that in your home, but he wants to stay in shape for it anyway. This activity is a great way to create a breeze on a warm day. Frequent or vigorous cockatiel wing activity is sure to blow powdered feed and dust and cage debris all over. Good thing you know enough to have a vacuum handy if you keep a cockatiel!

If your cockatiel isn't doing his exercises often, you can help him keep in shape by holding onto his feet and taking him "flying" around the room, or up and down in place, to generate lots of flapping activity. This is supposed to be a fun activity for both of you, so introduce it gently and make sure that you're obvious about having a good time!

Molting

The process of molting is both interesting and confusing. First of all, birds don't lose *all* their feathers at once when they molt. Cockatiels tend to molt twice a year: in the spring and again in the fall. More frequent molts can be triggered by a warm environment or by the number of hours per day a cockatiel is awake. When a bird molts, he replaces his feathers systematically over a period of time. In cockatiels, this period lasts about six weeks to two months. Molting starts with the feathers on the head, and ends with the long tail feathers. In other parrot species, molting may be normal only once a year or even once every two years. During the molt, your job is to keep sweeping up feathers. You'll probably wonder how one small bird can generate so much fluff!

Feathers aren't distributed evenly over a cockatiel's body the way hair is on our furrier companions. Feathers grow in tracts that are arranged so that appropriate feathers can do their job. The feather tracts are called *pterylae*. Bare areas between them are called *apteria*.

Anatomy of the molt

Here is a list of the kinds of feathers that your cockatiel will shed and grow anew during its molt. Not all feathers are created equal. Some are made to disintegrate, some enable flight, and others give shape to your cockatiel.

- ✔ **Contour feathers:** These are the most numerous type of feathers on a cockatiel's body. They're compact feathers with puffy fluffs at their base and harder, interlocking barbs at the tip, with a stiff central shaft. Contour feathers define the outer cockatiel that you see.

- ✔ **Covert feathers:** These small contour feathers are found on the wings and tail of your cockatiel, lined up in rows above the longer flight feathers of these appendages.

- ✔ **Down feathers:** These feathers don't have a shaft and form a warm layer under the contour feathers. When a cockatiel is just hatched, he only has down feathers, white or yellow fluff that begins to be replaced with real feathers at 10 to 14 days old.

- ✔ **Flight feathers:** Found on both the wings and in the tail, these feathers have special names depending on their location. Flight feathers of the wing are called *remiges,* and flight feathers of the tail are called *retrices.*

- ✔ **Powder down feathers:** These feathers are meant to disintegrate and spread keratin dust. They are not found in every parrot, but cockatiels are one of the birds in which powder down feathers exist. Other parrots native to arid environments, such as cockatoos and African grey parrots, also have powder down feathers.

- ✔ **Remiges:** These long, stiff feathers of the wing make flight possible. The flight feathers closest to a cockatiel's body are called the *secondaries.* Long flight feathers on the outside of the wing are called the *primaries* and are the feathers that are often clipped short in order to curtail a cockatiel's flight indoors. Remiges are usually asymmetrical in shape and have little or no down at their base.

- ✔ **Retrices:** These flight feathers are found in the tail. They are often symmetrical feathers of varying lengths and do indeed play a very big part in a cockatiel's aerodynamic abilities.

The molting process

New feathers are called *pin feathers* and are encased in a plastic-looking keratin sheath. The pin feathers have a blood supply and nerves. Any damage to the incoming feather causes pain and bleeding. The fastest way to stop the bleeding is to pull the feather. (Most broken blood feathers are wing or tail feathers. Use a pliers for the wing, but a quick jerk near the base will pull out a tail feather.) Feathers grow from the base upward and outward from a feather follicle in your cockatiel's skin. The tip of a feather is mature and will unfurl from its protective sheath, while the base is still connected to a blood supply and is still maturing. A molt happens when new feathers begin to grow in.

A cockatiel that is stressed by illness or malnutrition may not molt normally or may only partially molt. Molting requires extra energy and nutrients that an ill bird may not be able to afford to put into it. Sometimes stress during the molt shows up as stress lines in new feathers.

A cockatiel can usually unfurl his own keratin sheaths from pin feathers but may appreciate some help with his head feathers, where he can't reach to groom himself. If your cockatiel has not allowed you to scratch or groom his head before, this is a good time of year to teach him this behavior. Get him used to pressure on his head by blowing on his feathers. As he gets used to that slight pressure, occasionally use a finger to pet his head lightly. Eventually, you should be able to groom his head feathers and run your finger against the grain of his feathers on his head, just behind his crest. You're really won him over when he lowers his head for a scratch when he sees you!

A cockatiel can still fly while he's molting. He loses only a few feathers at a time, and loses pairs of flight feathers in its wing and tail in succession so that he doesn't lose the ability to fly or to keep himself warm and dry. As flight feathers grow in on his wings, a cockatiel regains the ability to fly. Keep close track of these feathers and note when it's time to have the wing feathers trimmed, as discussed in Chapter 6.

Your cockatiel will appreciate a little nutritional boost at this time of year. He'll probably chew on cuttlebone or mineral block for extra calcium (see Chapter 5) and appreciate added sources of protein as well. Try some scrambled egg, hard-cooked egg, frozen thawed peas, flaked chicken, tuna, or some pellets made for breeding birds, which contain extra protein and calcium.

A cockatiel of a different color

At the first molt, juvenile cockatiels start acquiring adult coloring. Females do not change color; they grow in feathers that are the same color as the set they had as babies. Male cockatiels, however, grow in solid yellow or white heads and solid-colored tail feathers. In the case of pearl mutation cockatiels, the males start to lose their pearl markings at the first molt as they become solid-colored birds rather than birds with fancy markings. Pied male cockatiels usually don't change color or pattern when they molt; as a result, determining their sex based on their appearance is difficult.

If you keep your household environment exceptionally warm, or if your cockatiel moves between households with vastly different temperatures, your cockatiel may be stimulated to molt more often than twice a year, as is normal.

Night Frights

Cockatiels are even-tempered pets and rarely flighty. Cockatiel owners are often shocked, therefore, to wake up to a cockatiel in an obvious panic, beating himself against the bars of his cage. This experience is not at all uncommon among cockatiel owners. Your cockatiel will have occasional episodes of wild night thrashing. Once you realize that night thrashing is peculiar to cockatiels and have ways to deal with it, you will no longer panic when your pet does!

All cockatiel owners can expect to experience some night thrashing with their pet birds. The color of the cockatiel involved may make a difference in the amount of night thrashing you have to endure. Lutino cockatiels can be beautiful, but have been so heavily inbred that they have several problems. A genetic baldness behind the crest is one problem, and incidences of night thrashing is another. If thrashing does occur, lutinos and pied cockatiels are the most likely to break blood feathers in the melee. If you insist on having a lutino, look for one with no bald spot and ask about a potential pet's parents. You'll want to hear that they're even-tempered birds who are friendly pets with a minimum of health or feather problems. (See more about cockatiel mutation colors in Chapter 1).

When a cockatiel is away from home — at a show or in a classroom, at a pet store, or at a boarding facility — the evidence of night thrashing is often blood splattered all over a cage and surrounding area. Warn your cockatiel's caretaker so he knows to check for continued bleeding. It's also a good idea to ask pet sitters to read this book so that they know what to expect from your cockatiel.

Possible reasons for thrashing

Many possible causes of night thrashing have been proposed over the years. A bird may feel vulnerable and helpless in the dark. Birds see colors well, but cockatiels are essentially blind at night. This is why a cockatiel quiets down, in most cases, when his cage is covered. When startled at night, then, a cockatiel responds by flailing wildly about his cage. If several cockatiels are in one cage or one room, the flock instinct takes over, and they all start thrashing about. The trigger can be one of many things.

Mice may be getting into your bird cage or cages. Mice love bird feed as much as birds do and are even more prolific. Because mouse droppings could be laced with the *E. coli* bacteria, causing sickness in a bird who ingested it, you don't want mice around. Start by removing the temptation; take out the feed dishes overnight when mice are active and replace them in the day when vermin are sleeping and your bird likes to be eating.

If you live in certain parts of the country, cockatiels are natural earthquake alarms. They sense even mild quakes that people do not feel, so this sensation may cause night thrashing. You'll have to read the papers or search the Internet to find out what your bird was fussing about.

Another catalyst for night thrashing is unfamiliar surroundings. Cockatiels being boarded frighten easily for the first few days they're away from home. Unfamiliar sights and sounds trigger panic and thrashing. If you intend to travel with your pet cockatiel or to board him at someone else's home, consider getting into the habit of covering your bird's cage. He will feel more secure while away from home if he has familiar nighttime scenery. Be sure a sitter knows what the bird is used to and when bedtime is.

Though there is no one reason we can pinpoint for night thrashing, cockatiels probably aren't prone to nightmares. Rather, spiders or insects may startle them and then flit away before being discovered. A bird may bump into a toy in the middle of the night or may detect an unfamiliar movement. Prevention is fairly simple. If you keep a night light on @ a child's night light works fine — near a cockatiel's cage, he can see when startled, instead of floundering blindly about its cage.

Responding to a thrashing episode

When night thrashing does occur, your response should be to calmly get up and turn the light on so your bird can see once again. Then start to talk softly to your cockatiel. He should begin to calm down when he hears your voice. A frightened cockatiel has a very erect crest and sits high on his perch, glancing nervously around. He looks tall and skinny, with all his feathers held tightly to his body. He may be clinging to the side bars of his cage, crest up and tail fanned out. When calming down, his crest will go down, and he may start to grate his beak in preparation for going back to sleep.

You may need to administer first aid to your bird. Look at him carefully and check the cage floor for signs of blood. During molting, a cockatiel may break blood feathers when thrashing about. The molt puts you in a sort of no-win situation regarding thrashing. Molting birds just don't feel well in general. They may be quicker to panic at night and do more harm to their growing feathers.

I keep some common items on hand for such emergencies. Some blood coagulant (in the form of styptic powder or pencils available at pet stores and pharmacies) or a box of cornstarch will help stop the bleeding. In a pinch, you can use flour. Apply one of these items, along with some light pressure, to the affected area until the bleeding stops. You can use tweezers to pull out a blood feather. Tail feathers pull out easily and painlessly in one quick jerk, but you need tweezers to grasp and pull out wing feathers. If a broken blood feather is left in place, it will continue to siphon off blood. The flow will stop if you remove the broken shaft of the blood feather. You may very well need veterinary help to remove a feather from a cockatiel's wing, as its wing bones need to be supported during this procedure, and you don't want to make a mistake that could injure your pet. A towel completes a good thrashing preparedness kit, for use in restraining frightened cockatiels.

Most damage from thrashing is minor, and it is rarely necessary to take a thrashing cockatiel to a vet. Damage may be minor but *look* horrible because blood may spatter on the cage and nearby walls.

Day thrashing

Thrashing doesn't have to occur only at night. Most often it does, but if a cockatiel sees unfamiliar clothing, a hat, or his first moustache on a human being, that can trigger the same response in daylight. A color, a patterned shirt, or a new person in the bird's environment could set off your cockatiel. Learn to think like a bird to discover what's different to a cockatiel with highly developed senses of sight and hearing. Maybe you like your new hair color, but your cockatiel may have a different opinion to express!

There is potential for serious injury to a thrashing bird, however, so it's a good policy to get up and check on your pet when you hear him thrashing. Bands can get caught on loose wires, and heads or wings may get caught in cage bars. You should inspect your cage for safety a couple times a year, possibly remove bands from a companion cockatiel, repair any loose wires in a cage, or even replace an aging cage.

REMEMBER

Establish a good relationship with a local avian veterinarian so that you know where to take your cockatiel in an emergency.

Once a thrashing bird has been calmed, you can usually leave him with only a night light. If your cockatiel has frequent incidents of night thrashing, carefully observe the room for signs of mice, bugs, or alarming movement so you know what steps to take to prevent another incident. You may need to move favorite toys to places where your cockatiel can't bump into them at night.

Vocalizations

A cockatiel uses vocalizations that you will probably come to know as expressing mood or wishes. They range in decibel level and pitch. Cockatiel vocalizations mostly consist of the calls a cockatiel may use to communicate with his flockmates in the wild. These calls let her flock know where he is or ask where they are. They warn of danger, communicate caring and bonding, or call for dinner.

Of course, one of the ultimate vocalizations you expect from a parrot is intelligible words. Cockatiels are not known for their talking ability, but a male cockatiel in a verbal household may indeed pick up the language of its human flock. You can't expect this degree of verbalization from a female cockatiel.

Grating beaks are grating

You may like knowing your cockatiel is contented when you hear him grind his beak, but you may never like the sound itself! Usually a cockatiel grinds his beak as he drifts off to sleep. Grating is a sound of contentment in a cockatiel; it's a happy sound! You may not especially enjoy this contented grating, though. Many people say that it has the same effect as fingernails on a chalkboard. The sound may make you want to gnash your teeth, scream in pain, or exit the premises. Instead, try to enjoy your cockatiel's happiness.

Gargling

When a cockatiel is interested in learning human speech, a phrase doesn't just pop out of his mouth fully formed and intelligible. The first stages of talking for a companion bird consist of an attempt to imitate the intonation of a phrase. It kind of sounds like gargling when he's just using gibberish. If you recognize the intonation and want to encourage your cockatiel to talk, praise him and respond to him when he's talking. Eventually, he'll enunciate more clearly. Your male bird is most likely to succeed in talking.

Whistling

Male cockatiels can become expert whistlers. The wolf whistle is practically a natural call for a cockatiel; most of them master it. Of course, the more inspiration you give your cockatiel, the more expert he will become. Play music for him, sing to him, and whistle your favorite tunes. A cockatiel parrot has a certain amount of behavior and calls that are instinctual. Scientists are discovering that another whole set of vocalizations are learned in parrots. This means that while your cockatiel is young, he is very receptive to learning the flock language at your house.

A cockatiel will learn the whistles and vocalizations he hears in your house. If you whistle or sing off-key, guess what your willing pupil will learn? Use language you want repeated and have the family musician give singing lessons to your talented male cockatiel!

Once again, the ladies don't learn exuberant vocalizations. Their strength is their loving, gentle ways, and they express their joy and love in softer tones.

Sweet nothings

Cockatiels express their love for you in various ways. When they confuse their affection for you with the sexual advances they would make to a mate, you may hear some new vocalizations. Mature female cockatiels solicit a male quite vocally. They make their body level, with their wings out to the side and tail raised, and make a continuing, soft vocalization that is best described as a "rolling coo." It is unlike any of the normal clucks and screams you hear from a cockatiel, and it means she's in the mood. This isn't a mood you necessarily want to encourage, so ignore her behavior or divert her attention with a toy or some other activity that encourages a change in behavior.

Male cockatiels who like a female cockatiel show their sentiments by whistling loudly in her ear. If you're the object of your male cockatiel's affection, you'll get the same treatment. A male cockatiel's sweet nothings are loud and enthusiastic.

Hisssss! I'm a snake! Aren't you scared?

The ultimate cockatiel defense when he's scared or not in the mood to meet you is a hiss. Chicks in a nest use this as their defense from intruders into their nest box. The effect is that of a reptile and may make you believe — as scientists do — that there is a close association between dinosaurs and birds.

Toy obsessions

A cockatiel left alone to his own devices in his cage comes up with some interesting diversions. When toys are their only companions in a cage, your cockatiel may take a liking to one or come up with unusual uses for it. If your cockatiel has a bell, he may very well develop the common cockatiel habit of "wearing" his bell while he's sleeping. He goes up under a bell and puts it on his head like a cap in this case. Other cockatiels learn to warble into the bell for a nice echo effect — they're the natural-born entertainers of the flock.

Another behavior that's more disturbing for owners is a male cockatiel's masturbating on a toy in a cage. He does so by rubbing his vent on the object of his affection. Because the bird has no other sexual outlet, you could encounter this behavior in your companion cockatiel. Discourage the behavior by not giving the cockatiel a lot of attention for it. Don't say anything, and turn away when the cockatiel is masturbating. Your attention, affection, and verbalizations are encouraging to him.

You might also consider cutting out behavior that stimulates sexual excitement in your cockatiel. Keep daylight hours to 10 to 12 hours per day. Fifteen hours stimulates breeding behavior. Other breeding stimuli include access to a nesting site, which is any dark area such as a shelf, shoebox, birdie house, or enclosed toy. Because you're probably the mate to which your cockatiel is bonded, minimizing affectionate behavior and stroking may lower your cockatiel's hormone level as well.

You may encounter this hissing reaction from a cockatiel when you approach him but he doesn't want to meet you. You'll also hear this vocalization from a cockatiel if you corner him and insist on picking him up, but he really doesn't want you to handle him. A cockatiel may hiss if he has just been woken up from a nap or if you rapidly remove a cage cover and he doesn't quite realize how the dim-to-bright light transition is happening so fast. Unless you know a hissing cockatiel well and can remind him that you're a friend, a hiss is a good indication that he will bite you.

A hissing cockatiel is saying, "Don't touch me" or "Don't you dare." He's prepared to use the fight of his fight-or-flight instincts because he's been surprised or has no flight alternative in this situation. A few perpetually grumpy or resolutely untame cockatiels hiss often, while others never use this vocalization at all. Hissing can be accompanied by a slow swaying from side to side, like a snake about to strike. You've been forewarned.

Watch the Birdie

Developing a close and mutually affectionate relationship with your cockatiel involves some cross-species communication. With close observation, you can learn to read your cockatiel's moods and react accordingly. Reassure your cockatiel when he's frightened, and be ready to play when things are going great. You can make adjustments in your environment if you see something is scaring your cockatiel. Over time, you'll start to find out how a cockatiel asks for food, water, or attention. Watching your cockatiel and making mental notes of the body language he uses in various situations is a good way to foster communication. Developing communication furthers affection, which is all the reason in the world for both you and your cockatiel to be observant of each other.

Cockatiels express mood with various parts of their body. Watch their feathers. Cockatiels can lift up each feather, fluff their feathers to look big, or pull their feathers tightly to their body. Watch a cockatiel's wings. Are they relaxed, spread wide, or held over his head? Watch a cockatiel's crest for some indication of mood — a crest isn't just a hood ornament. Finally, consider how a cockatiel is holding his body. Is he relaxed, tense, combative, or strutting his stuff?

Crest placement tells moods

A cockatiel's crest is relatively short when he's young, and it tends to stay upright more often than it does in older, wiser cockatiels. This gives the impression that youngsters are always startled, if you know how to read a cockatiel crest. An upright crest means that a cockatiel is frightened or startled by what's happening. A cockatiel who is relaxed has his crest lying loosely and flat on his head, with only the end curling up. A cockatiel who wants your attention flattens his crest and wavers his wings, perhaps pacing side to side until he gets your attention. An angry cockatiel may make a challenge with his crest up, but if he's serious about biting, he'll put his crest down and go for it. If you pass by your cockatiel's cage, he'll probably put his crest up higher than "relaxed" but not as far up as "startle." Cockatiel calibration hasn't been perfected, but with frequent observation, you'll soon understand the various levels of crest placement.

Communication through body language

Cockatiels slick their feathers to their body when they're frightened. They want to be a small target in case there's a risk of being caught by a predator. A frightened cockatiel stands tall and is very alert and vigilant, ready to fly from danger. Cockatiels also have very slicked-down feathers when they're too hot. Then they open their mouth to pant, and hold their wings out from their side. A cockatiel who is this hot would love a cool shower.

An angry cockatiel advances with slick feathers and his neck stuck out, ready to bite or beak-wrestle with an adversary. Cockatiels open their mouths and tussle with their beaks when they're having a disagreement. Parakeets boink beaks for fun.

A cockatiel who is comfortable sits low on his perch, and his feathers lie loosely on his body. He may be comfortable enough to lower his guard and tuck his beak into his back for a cockatiel nap.

If your cockatiel is looking for some cuddling and preening, he'll lower his neck and head, waiting. Perhaps he'll even press his head to your cheek to ask you to preen him. You can lower your head to your cockatiel if your hair needs preening.

A cockatiel loving his bath spreads his wings and fans every feather out from his body to catch all the water droplets. For another reason, a cockatiel who wants to appear large and dominant in his territory raises all the feathers on his body and raise his wings.

A cockatiel who is ill fluffs his feathers out from his body, taking full advantage of the soft coat of down feathers to help him retain body heat. A seriously ill cockatiel or a hen in labor with an egg may sit on the floor of the cage as well.

Hours of entertainment

Observing your cockatiel isn't work, so you'll catch yourself watching your cockatiel's antics many times when you should be doing some task that is less fun than bird watching! It's a triumphant feeling when you realize for the first time that you understand what your cockatiel is communicating and can respond to it. With any luck, a few of your lessons — such as teaching what "up" means and when meal times and play time happens at your house — are getting through to your cockatiel as well. As the years pass, you'll know what behavior is normal for your cockatiel in different seasons, and you'll figure out how to tell his likes and dislikes as well as moods. Of course, a cockatiel who wolf whistles at your friends and grooms their moustaches is not being too subtle in his communication!

If your companion cockatiel wants to be with you, he paces back and forth in his cage, calling to you. He may also lean out from the cage and quiver his wings, all but flying to you.

An agitated cockatiel calls and paces. This may mean "I don't have any water," "You're late with breakfast, and I don't know what a weekend is," or "Give me one of those crackers!"

Chapter 10

Training Your Cockatiel to Be an Outstanding Companion

In This Chapter
▶ Calling in the professionals
▶ Checking out books and Web sites about parrot behavior
▶ Teaching commands
▶ Socializing your cockatiel

Shaping and modifying your cockatiel's behavior is a long-term but fulfilling project. Training involves using your observation skills and thinking about the behavior of both yourself and your companion cockatiel. Your gut reactions to a behavior often reward bad behavior and encourage the behavior. You must make a conscious effort to behave in a way that rewards good behavior and ignores or changes bad behavior.

The very best thing you can do for both yourself and your cockatiel is to cultivate good habits in your young cockatiel or the older cockatiel who is new to you. Changing ingrained behavior is much more difficult than thoughtfully and consistently shaping your cockatiel's behavior so that she is a good bird citizen and adapts well to life in a human household. Good behavior doesn't come naturally to your bird. As cute and forgiving and cheerful as a cockatiel is, she's meant to fly, forage, and procreate. Your hope is that your cockatiel will give and receive your love and entertain you with her antics.

Your cockatiel is a living being with opinions, instincts, and a penchant for throwing around food and making messes. You can have an incredible, fun adventure as you explore the possibilities for communication and behavior modification based on respect and understanding. And when you cockatiel is getting on your nerves, think about the challenge and the fun and joys of having a cockatiel. You could live without her screaming for your attention at times, but could you live without her cheerful voice in the morning, the chance to share toast for breakfast, or her greeting when you come home in the evening? Make all your moments together count.

Working with a Bird Behaviorist

If you need guidance in shaping the behavior of your young cockatiel, you may want to hire a professional. Bird behaviorists specialize in working with parrots and their families to modify behavior so that a household is more peaceful.

Where to find a behaviorist

Parrot behaviorists don't need to have a degree or complete a certification program to practice. Some people have hung out their shingle to do this work and stay in the field when they have success with it. There are relatively few parrot behaviorists in the country; you can't necessarily expect to find one in your community. The good news is that their numbers are growing! The best way to find a behaviorist is to get a referral from a happy client. Try asking your avian veterinarian or bird club members about their experience. If you're fortunate, maybe someone in your community is a bird behavior expert who can offer an in-home consultation.

Parrot behaviorists are listed in bird magazines and on the Internet. If you can't find local help, it's time to get long-distance help by consulting an expert over the phone. Be prepared to describe your bird, her behavior, and her daily routine in great detail. Call the behaviorist at the times she requests, keeping in mind that you may be in different time zones. You're paying a premium for an expert's experience and advice, so be sure to follow it, or at least don't complain about your results if you don't! And pay promptly, out of respect and professionalism.

What to expect

Consultations may happen in person on the phone. A professional parrot behaviorist will ask you many questions about the problems you're having with your cockatiel, her routine, when problems occur, and maybe some of the dynamics of the household. It's helpful for a consultant to actually meet you and your bird. Doing so allows her to observe the cockatiel's surroundings and how she interacts with a family. Often a behaviorist can show you handling techniques that improve the relationship between a cockatiel and her owners. Obviously, calling in an expert at the first sign of unwanted behavior can turn around the relationship you create between your cockatiel and your family.

Most behavioral issues don't have quick fixes. Expect to be working on modification of a behavior for several weeks to months, until you gradually have modified an unwanted behavior. If you call in a professional and pay for her opinion, it still is up to you to implement the advice. You must be consistent in performing new behaviors and adopting new attitudes requested by your behavioral consultant. Take note that a parrot behaviorist will be working with both you and your cockatiel. You'll both have new behaviors to learn.

Educating Yourself

Read as much as you can about companion parrot behavior. Your cockatiel is a parrot, and most of the same principles apply. You'll get ideas from behavior books about how to interact with and play with your cockatiel. Pay special attention to what the experts have to say about cockatoo behavior, as cockatiels are cousins to the cockatoos. Opinions vary on how best to prevent, cope with, or correct companion parrot behavior.

Your cockatiel is a special parrot in that she is native (along with budgies) to the Australian desert and not the rain forest. Read all you can about parrot behavior and apply what seems reasonable for you and your bird, in your situation.

Good books

A few people have made outstanding contributions to the study of bird behavior and graciously share their knowledge through the books they have written and regular speaking engagements at educational seminars. An increasing number of educational classes are available about companion birds. Not all experts agree on technique, but I advise reading everything you can find. Read carefully and apply what seems to fit for you and your cockatiel in your situation.

Here are several books about bird behavior:

- *Abundantly Avian* by Phoebe Greene Linden: This book is very sensitive, observant, and intellectual. Phoebe, a parrot breeder, was the first to use the phrase "abundance weaning" and to write and speak about an avian adolescence.

- *The Alex Studies* by Dr. Irene Maxine Pepperberg: Covers more than 20 years of landmark research about the intelligence of parrots. Alex, an African grey parrot who has been the focus of parrot intelligence research, has learned to label colors, shapes, matter, and same/different and has tested at the same level of intelligence as dolphins and chimps.

- *Birds For Dummies* by Gina Spadafori and Brian L. Speer, DVM: Covers the basics of bird care with wit and clarity. Dr. Speer is one of the foremost avian veterinarians, so the medical information in this book is state-of-the art and comprehensive.

- ✔ *The Complete Book of Cockatiels* by me, Diane Grindol: Meant to be the standard cockatiel book everyone should have. Includes findings from cockatiel research at the University of California Davis, and my experience from 15 years of cockatiel care. In color, with stories about real cockatiel owners and experts in nutrition and genetics.

- ✔ *Guide to a Well-Behaved Parrot* by Mattie Sue Athan: One of the first and most popular books about parrot behavior. Thoroughly covers the basics.

- ✔ *Handbook of Avian Articles* by Liz Wilson: Articles written by a parrot behavioral consultant who is also a veterinary technician and has lived with a blue-and-gold macaw for 26 years. This is a self-published book. Write for more info: Liz Wilson, 64 Jonquil Lane, Levittown, PA 19055 or visit www3.upatsix.com/liz/book.html.

- ✔ *My Parrot, My Friend* by Bonnie Munro Doane: Another one of the standard, first extensively researched books on parrot behavior.

- ✔ *Parrot Companion Handbook* by Sally Blanchard: Founder of the Pet Bird Report magazine and mostly responsible for the acceptance of "parrot behaviorist" as a profession, Sally has devoted her life to spreading information that promotes understanding between people and parrots. Her book is full of suggestions for raising a well-adjusted parrot.

- ✔ *Parrots . . . Parrots . . . Parrots!* by Layne David Dicker: Layne spends time in a veterinary office for parrot behavior consultations. He appreciates cockatiels, and his writing style is vastly entertaining. All proceeds benefit the Parrot Education and Adoption Center (PEAC) in San Diego. Order the book at or write Parrot Education & Adoption Center (PEAC), P.O. Box 600423, San Diego, CA 92160.

- ✔ *The Pleasure of Their Company* by Bonnie Munro Doane: More about parrot behavior, with training suggestions.

Helpful Web sites

The Internet is a great source of information. A good place to start is a search engine such as www.yahoo.com or www.altavista.com. Look for topics such as cockatiels, parrots, and parrot behavior.

Here are some Web pages that I like that are dedicated to cockatiels and other types of parrots:

- ✔ North American Cockatiels Society: www.cockatiel.org/. Founded to meet the needs of companion cockatiel owners. You'll find links, tips, and referrals to avian veterinarians, articles, and a chat board. Why not nominate your cockatiel as "Pet Cockatiel of the Month"?

✔ We're Parrots Too: `www.ashlandcreative.com/wpt/`. This site is for the little avicultural wonders: cockatiels, parakeets, and lovebirds. A good resource for articles and links, and a graphically rich site.

✔ National Cockatiel Society: `www.cockatiels.org/`. Find out about cockatiel exhibitions. Learn about color mutations and breeding, and search for a cockatiel through the classifieds.

✔ Australian National Cockatiel Society, Inc.: `www.bit.net.au/~ancs/`. Articles and links from cockatiel fanciers "down under."

✔ American Cockatiel Society: `www.acstiels.com/`. Includes lists of shows, articles, and a chance to ask cockatiel questions.

✔ Up At Six: `www.upatsix.com`. A site loaded with pet bird care and information, as well as links to many of the bird chats available. Includes the `rec.pets.birds` FAQ (Frequently Asked Questions) and serves as a behavior resource. There's even some fun stuff on this site.

✔ The Pet Bird Report: `www.petbirdreport.com`. The ultimate meeting place if you really get into bird behavior. You'll find Sally Blanchard's speaking schedule posted and may be able to locate a parrot behaviorist near you.

Training at Home

It takes patience and consistency to train your cockatiel. The rewards are increased communication between you and your cockatiel. There are some basic behaviors that are really helpful to teach your cockatiel to make everyday life easier. One of these is the Up command. This is a basic bird command akin to Sit, Down, and Stay for a companion dog. At the word "up," you can teach a cockatiel to step onto your finger or a stick. It's good for you to get your cockatiel out of his cage on a daily basis. When going back in the cage is quick and easy, then you'll both continue the practice. In this section, I look at some of the ways to train your cockatiel to quietly enter and exit his cage as well as to learn to hop up at your command.

Teaching the Up command

Cockatiels are bright animals. They learn behaviors quickly when they're taught lovingly and consistently. You can teach a cockatiel to understand the principle of the Up command in a single lesson. It then just takes practice so that a cockatiel's response to the command becomes automatic.

The command to get up on your finger is a vital communication between you and your cockatiel. After your cockatiel understands the verbal command, you won't have to poke at her or chase her and then grab or suddenly force her onto a finger. Instead, your cockatiel will be ready and usually willing to step on your finger. Even if she's not especially willing, obeying the Up command becomes a habit after a while. When your cockatiel knows that she must obey this command, you can use it in many situations. For example, use it when she's on your shoulder and would prefer to stay there forever. The Up command also comes in handy if your cockatiel is throwing a hissy fit and needs to diffuse her emotions and be distracted by doing something praiseworthy. Then you can both calm down.

You don't have to use the word "up" when training a cockatiel to get on your finger. Your cockatiel associates a command with the action of getting on your finger, but doesn't come to understand the meaning of "up" as a word. She's simply consistently heard that word for stepping up. You could just as easily whistle, cluck, snap your fingers, or use the word "rhubarb" for a command meaning to step up on your finger. Variations people use include "step up," "come," and "perch."

For the sake of convention, I advise using the word "up." "Up" was popularized by Sally Blanchard in her bird behavior articles and consultations, and it's become a standard in bird training. Most birds, as long-lived as they are, live in several households during their life. If a cockatiel is ever lost or placed in a new household, knowing the common Up command will make her feel much more at home, and new owners will be able to tell that the bird was trained by conscientious people.

Here's how you teach your cockatiel the Up command:

1. **Get your cockatiel out of her cage.**

   Eventually, you'll be able to use the Up command for this. Till then, open the cage door and let your cockatiel come out, or grab her with a towel or your hands.

2. **Take her to neutral space, out of sight of her cage, and put her down on a surface, even on the floor.**

3. **Use one hand to guide your cockatiel from behind, and press the index finger of the other hand into the cockatiel's chest above her feet, as shown in Figure 10-1. Push her up gently from behind to start, so that she perches on your index finger.**

4. **Start a ladder of Up commands over and over (see Figure 10-2).**

   Force your cockatiel to obey at first. Now that she's on one of your index fingers, rotate that finger backwards slowly and subtly to knock your cockatiel off balance. At about the same time, push the index finger of your other hand up onto your bird's chest above her feet. She'll sense there's somewhere steady to go and will step up. Say "up" as your cockatiel is stepping onto the new finger.

Figure 10-1:
Getting in
position to
attempt
the Up
command.

Figure 10-2:
The
cockatiel
climbs onto
the next
finger.

A cockatiel will want to get up off the floor and on to a higher perch. You can give her what she wants and train her at the same time by practicing Up commands that get her progressively higher till you're looking each other in the face. That's quite a reward!

5. **Keep repeating the command "up" consistently as your cockatiel steps onto your finger.**

    After a few tries, she should be raising her foot to step up or following the command on her own.

    If your cockatiel flies off your finger, start over from where she lands.

    Praise her during the training routine.

Practice this training routine for a few minutes whenever you get your cockatiel out and repeat it until Up is a command she knows and understands. You also want to teach your cockatiel that she must obey this command. Don't let her refuse to step up once you've asked her to. If she just sits there, use both hands and make her get up.

A cockatiel will learn to respond to any spoken, whistled, verbalized, or signaled command you choose to mean to step up onto your finger. The Up command has become conventional, though, and will be less confusing to other companion bird lovers.

Teaching the Up command can lead easily to teaching other behaviors. When your cockatiel learns to automatically reach up when you say "up," you can give her a command for "wave." You can teach her to come and get up on your finger from across the room, starting with small distances and gradually lengthening the distance your cockatiel must walk or fly to you.

Troubleshooting the Up command

The Up command is one of the most useful behaviors for fostering communication and understanding with our cockatiels. But not all cockatiels take to it immediately, especially if they're older or shy. A hissing cockatiel who won't come near you isn't going to learn to step up on your finger in 15 minutes, but over time, you can train your reticent cockatiel that she can be handled and can train her to respond to a couple commands. Allow yourself several months to win over a resistant cockatiel.

Another branch of the family

There's no rule saying that you have to use the Up command to get a bird on your finger. If your cockatiel bites down on a finger when it is offered to her, or your cockatiel won't come near a finger, you can train your cockatiel to step up onto a perch, stick, or ladder. That variation still gives you control and gives many cockatiels the personal space they need to distance themselves from human contact. Start by letting the cockatiel get used to your stick or ladder — nonthreatening, inanimate objects — lying on the cage.

Next, offer your cockatiel the stick, pressing it up against her chest and pretty much forcing her to get on. As she jumps on, say "up." Praise her and tell her how good she is! Gradually, move her and the stick so that you can use this command to return her to her cage or move her somewhere. Practice this action several times a day and thank your cockatiel profusely for cooperating with you!

If she goes, I go

Try using pair bonding to modify behavior. Use what works! If you have two cockatiels who like to be together, chances are good that they want to be doing the same thing most of the time. If one of the cockatiels is tame and willing to step up for you, she can help you train a second, less tame cockatiel. Ask your tame cockatiel to get on your finger and start lifting her up towards you.

Your cockatiel's friend should be straining to follow. Give her a leg up by offering her your finger, stick, or ladder to step onto, and maybe she'll take you up on the offer of a ride. If this technique works for you, start saying "up" to the cockatiel who usually only follows the lead of her companion. After a couple weeks, ask her to step up first to see whether she's learned the command.

When you teach an untame cockatiel to step up, you're teaching her a behavior that makes your mutual relationship easier. Your goal is not to win pet of the month or to suddenly expect this resistant cockatiel to love you. You're just working it out so that you can live together and communicate on some level. If you have more than one cockatiel and their relationship is more adversarial than friendly, you can use that too. Within full view of one of the cockatiels, ask the tamer one to step up and give her lots of attention. Do this several times so her jealous rival sees exactly what's going on. Now give the jealous cockatiel the Up command. If she doesn't step up, show her again how it's done, with her rival, and praise her exuberantly. Maybe take her into a different room or feed her a real treat, like a sunflower seed. Doing that should drive your jealous bird wild. Even if you don't get immediate cooperation, try this over and over a few times to see whether she's catching on. Her attitude should be "I want what she's got!"

Bait and switch

If you have an unfriendly, single cockatiel, you may want to use both hands for the Up command. Use one hand as bait for a cockatiel whose reaction to your hand in front of her beak is to attack it. Offer the flat back of your hand or flat palm. You aren't really aiming to get bitten. Then with the other hand, press a finger firmly above her feet and into her chest, forcing her to step up for you. She'll hardly know how it all happened.

Approaching from behind

You want your cockatiel to behave wonderfully and to do a picture-perfect "up." If that's not happening for you, try the stealth approach. Many cockatiels are much more cooperative about stepping backwards when you come up behind — rather than in front of — them with your finger or a stick and ask them to step onto it. You're not as much of a target for the sharp beak, and you get the results you want. This approach is an option even for the tamest cocktails.

Coming and going

Your cockatiel can learn other behaviors faster once you've taught her the Up command. A behavior that is very helpful for a cockatiel to know is to quietly enter and exit her cage. This is a routine behavior, not necessarily associated with a command, but you certainly can chirp up with "lets go home," or "go back" when it's time for your cockatiel to go back to her cage. Follow these steps:

1. **Make sure that your cockatiel is outside the cage.**

   Review the Up command with her a couple times. She should be in a frame of mind to respond to you.

2. **Head towards the cage door.**

   With your cockatiel on your finger, hold her close to the cage door. Then bring her back to you. You're taking this step by step. This gets your cockatiel used to staying on your finger while heading for the cage. Be patient with her and be consistent in praising her for sitting quietly on your finger even when she is near her cage. Stop this exercise when your cockatiel has done this, before she gets tired or bored. Praise her!

3. **Praise your cockatiel.**

   This is great! Enthusiastically praise your cockatiel. Do this simple step for several days to a week, merely getting your cockatiel close to the cage. After a few times, allow your cockatiel to go back to playing. Stop while you have positive results and have been patient yourself.

4. **Next, with your cockatiel on your finger, calmly put her into and out of the cage, without actually giving her a chance to step off your finger onto a perch inside the cage.**

   You're getting her used to the action of exiting and entering her cage on your finger. Perform this action several times a day, for a few days, till she gets used to this new activity.

5. **Have your cockatiel get off onto a perch inside the cage, and then immediately ask her to step up onto your finger and exit the cage with her on your finger.**

Now practice this step. You're teaching your cockatiel both to get onto your finger to leave the cage and to enter it quietly.

6. **Try calmly putting your hand into your cockatiel's cage, and ask her to step up so that she can come out of the cage.**

   In this step you're asking your cockatiel to get on your hand when she is eating or playing, sleeping or preening; tending to her own business instead of stepping up in the middle of a training exercise. If she isn't ready yet, go back to earlier behaviors and keep working on them before trying the Up command inside her cage. A cockatiel's cage is her castle, retreat, and private space. It's a big deal for her to allow you to invade her space and to take her out of a secure place. Working on perfecting an easy exit, however, will be well worth the effort to you.

A behavior you can teach that is closely related to Up is the Off command for getting down off your finger onto a perch. There isn't a strict convention on this command. Try Off, Step off, Get down, or some other command that is meaningful to you and your cockatiel.

Going quietly back to the cage

Sometimes cockatiels don't like to go back to their cage when they've been out for a while, especially if you've been having fun and interacting with them. Do any of these behaviors sound familiar?

- ✔ **High-energy high-flying:** Some cockatiels start a game of hide-and-seek at bedtime. It's not that they're hidden, but they're out of reach on the curtain rods, the lampshades, and just one step ahead of where you can catch them. The harder you try, the farther they get.

- ✔ **Here again, gone again:** This cockatiel obediently comes onto your finger, but as you get near the cage or start heading in that direction, she's off and flying again. Let the games begin!

- ✔ **Grab and hold on:** You just about have your cockatiel in her cage, it looks like a done deal and then she grabs onto the bar at the top or side of the cage door and somehow ends up on top of the outside of her cage. This is a sneaky cockatiel.

- ✔ **I'm bigger than the cage door:** In a behavior similar to grab and hold on, a cockatiel has figured out that you can't fit her in her cage if she spreads her wings and doesn't fit through the door.

- ✔ **I'll just sleep here, thank you:** This cockatiel gets ahead because of her charm. She spends her evening cuddling up to you, preening your hair or moustache, and quietly falling asleep on your shoulder. You're too nice to wake her up and put her on a perch under a cover.

Your cockatiel also may exhibit these behaviors in the morning, when you let her out to play or socialize before you have to go to work. But before you leave, your cockatiel needs to return to her cage, so she can spend her day out of danger and near food and water. You're probably in a rush at this time of the day, so you've probably noticed that the more hurried you are about getting your cockatiel back in her cage, the harder it is to do. The first thing you need to do is calm down. The next thing that will help is judicious use of the Up command. Get your cockatiel on your finger.

A lot of minor comedies start out this way in cockatieldom. What you do next makes the difference, however. You want your cockatiel under your control; you don't want her to take off again, and you want to guide her into her cage. Calmly place your other hand very gently over your cockatiel's back. This action makes it impossible for your cockatiel to fly off. She can't open her wings to take off, and she can't open her wings to block the cage entrance. Guide her into the cage, and try to prevent her from grabbing the cage bar. Put her in backwards if you have to. Ask your cockatiel to step off your hand, and she's safely home. Practice this mild restraint at other times if it's not uncomfortable for your cockatiel.

Playing quietly alone

One favor you can do for your cockatiel in her first months at your house is to teach her to play quietly by herself. When you first bring your cockatiel home, you'll be enthralled with each other, and you may want to spend a great deal of time with her. Realistically, however, your normal routine is not cockatiel-centered. If your cockatiel knows how to play with toys and keep herself entertained in your absence, then you'll have a much better relationship.

One rule you can make about playtime is that your cockatiel should stay on a play gym, on a counter, or on the top of her cage. You can enforce the rule by being more persistent about it than your cockatiel can be about breaking it. Whenever your cockatiel leaves her designated play area, put her back there. Over and over again. Eventually she'll realize that you're a stickler for rules, and she'll give up trying to leave her play area or she'll test you only once in a while!

Although it's good exercise for your cockatiel to range freely outside her cage, it's dangerous. You risk stepping on your cockatiel, sitting on her, or slamming a door behind you if a loose cockatiel is following you. You should supervise your cockatiel when she's outside her cage, not allow her freedom all the time.

Expose your cockatiel early and often to the joys of playing with toys. Buy a variety of toys suitable for your cockatiel and turn everyday items into toys. Use your cockatiel's natural penchant for picking things up and chewing as well as their fascination with colors to keep a cockatiel entertained. Let her chew up mail you don't want to save, string Cheerios cereal on a shoelace, let her roll a bottle cap around, or pick at a new tissue. A busy cockatiel is a happy cockatiel.

The Adaptable Cockatiel

Cockatiels can get stuck in a rut easily. Exposing your cockatiel to a variety of situations and to a variety of people will help her be a more socially adjusted cockatiel and to accept new things as they come along. You can do this in a simple way by making it a practice to take your cockatiel with you into different rooms of your house. She'll get used to the variety of wall décor and furniture that way. Take her in or out of her cage. You can even set up bird playgrounds in each room so she can be with you if you have a reason to stay there for a while.

Introduce your cockatiels to your friends and family. Teach her to step off your hand onto someone else's hand if you request it and to be polite there! Remember that not everyone knows about birds. Show your friends how to pet your cockatiel and remind them that she likes shiny objects. Cockatiels find eyeglasses fascinating, too. People with glasses who meet a curious and outgoing cockatiel are likely to end up with a bird dangling from their frame. You be the judge of your friend's tolerance and control the situation!

Make sure that friends who socialize with your cockatiel know that she'll peck at jewelry. They may want to remove it before handling your cockatiel.

The purpose of meeting a lot of people is for your cockatiel to get used to the incredible variety of human appearances. Your cockatiel needs to see different colors of hair and skin and know that moustaches, beards, and eye shadow are normal. Socialization also helps your cockatiel accept the different accessories and clothing — from leopard skin to baseball caps — that people wear. You can extend your cockatiel's socialization by taking her to meetings or gatherings, as long as you ask for permission first. It is fine to take a cockatiel to classrooms and some to bird club meetings.

Children and the elderly have sensitive skin, so a cockatiel's toenails may cause them pain. Have these people pull their shirt sleeves down before holding a cockatiel. Or let them scratch your cockatiel's head while she sits on a T-stand, so they don't have to hold your cockatiel at all.

Chapter 11

What to Do about Problem Behaviors

*Y*ou may end up spoiling your cockatiel. He may acquire a habit that you consider annoying or problematic. Some people in your household may behave in a way that teaches your cockatiel unwanted behaviors.

If you acquire an older cockatiel, he'll come with both good and bad habits. Once a bad habit is acquired, you'll need to do some behavior modification in order to slowly influence your cockatiel to have good habits. Good habits are purely subjective and based on a person's point of view. From a cockatiel's perspective, a behavior that gets results is a keeper. He'll keep biting or screaming or stay bonded to a certain person if doing so gets him food or attention. He's programmed to live in a social flock, stay in touch with flock members, and spend a portion of every day foraging for food. Accompanying behaviors don't always fit into a human being's perception of good behaviors for a companion bird.

Despite the bad fit and enormous possibility of acquiring behaviors that people may consider bad, cockatiels have proven to be one of the most popular and resilient companion birds available to people. It's worth working with your cockatiel to change behavior and to come to an understanding you can both live with. It's worth not giving up. Too many cockatiels are turned over to adoption programs or given to a new household because their owners didn't take the time to work with the behaviors they had created. To avoid being an incriminating statistic, please give your cockatiel a chance to shine as a good companion in your home!

Screaming

Screaming is certainly not a cockatiel behavior you want to encourage. Cockatiels become closely bonded to their human companions and can fall into the pattern of screaming for attention whenever their favorite companion is not in sight. Your reaction to this may encourage a continuation of the behavior. Cockatiels are experts at training their family to come when they call. Cockatiels are family members, and in a loud family, they may have to be a loud bird to compete for attention in the household. There are times when a cockatiel is feeling his oats and can't help expressing himself verbally. The more you can do to recognize the meaning of a vocalization and to train yourself to reward communicative and not manipulative vocalizations, the better and more fulfilling your relationship with your cockatiel will be. It'll be a quieter relationship, too!

Preventing problem screaming

In one of the contradictory aspects of cockatiel ownership, one way to prevent problem screaming is to allow loud vocalizations. It's natural for a bird to vocalize, sometimes as loud as screaming, in the morning and evenings. Allow your bird to have these times for exuberant vocalizations. Enjoy your cockatiel's love for life and his expression of it.

Why birds vocalize

Screaming is one of a cockatiel's unpleasant vocalizations, so it's important to understand some basics of bird vocalizations. For starters, parrots in general are vocal creatures. That's one reason they're attractive to people, and one reason they're abandoned by people. People are such complex creatures themselves! They get what they want, and then they don't want it anymore because it's more than they bargained for.

Birds scream to warn of predators or to ward off an invasion of their territory. They scream when a flock is separated, until the flock is back together again. In the wild, birds do a lot of screaming in the morning as a flock wakes up and heads out to forage, and then again in the evening when the flock comes together to roost. Courtship is a noisy process, with males showing off their vocal abilities for potential mates.

Birds also scream for the sheer joy of it. One parrot vocalization researcher theorized that some parrots vocalize for the same reason people make music — for the joy and art of it. There's no doubt that some cockatiels are masters at complex vocalizations. Humans have a single voice box, but parrots have two vocal membranes and can imitate sounds that a person can't dream of achieving.

Another way to avoid problem vocalizations is to foster meaningful vocalizations. Cockatiels are meant to live in a flock, and you're a flock member. If a flock separates and its members are out of sight, they vocalize to stay in touch. This is called a contact call and is one of the most frequent parrot vocalizations. You can prevent problem, insistent screaming every time you walk out of the room by developing a contact call you exchange with your cockatiel. This can be a word or a whistle that means "Here I am."

Sometimes a person's response to a cockatiel scream is naturally a scream, especially if they're exasperated or annoyed by the vocalization. This attention and loud response is actually a reward for your cockatiel. If the bird screams and then you come in to the room and scream at him, what does your cockatiel get? Exactly what he wants, with added drama and entertainment. Cockatiels figure out quickly how to get their owners to appear. The verbal reward is icing on the cake. You can do two things to break the cycle. You can respond with a vocalization that reflects the model behavior you prefer from your cockatiel. For example, you can whisper or whistle when your cockatiel screams. Try it out.

Another way to prevent creating a screaming cockatiel and to maintain a quiet home is to give him positive reinforcement for being quiet. Obviously doing so takes some discipline on your part. When your cockatiel is quietly playing or patiently perched, give him attention, a favorite treat, and profuse praise.

Respond to nonverbal communications your cockatiel gives you so that his wishes don't escalate to loud demands. When your cockatiel obviously is asking for something, pay attention and fulfill the need. For example, maybe your cockatiel lets you know (when you sleep late in the morning!) that it's time for food by pacing back and forth and vocalizing. You can leave food in the cage overnight if your cockatiel needs breakfast before you wake up. If your cockatiel puts his head down, he may be requesting a scratch on the back of the head, some cuddling, and grooming time. If he paces back and forth or quivers his wings, he may want time with you, off his cage. Maybe your answer is "no" to a scritch or a ride on your shoulder right now, but at least acknowledge that to your cockatiel and tell him no, making his communication effective even though the answer wasn't the one he wanted.

When hormones are racing, your male cockatiel is likely to be his most vocal. This behavior is most likely in the spring and fall, when daylight hours stimulate a cockatiel to think about settling down and raising chicks. If you want to tone down that behavior, do the reverse of what you'd do to stimulate a pair of cockatiels to breed. Put your cockatiel to bed early, covering the cage after he's been up 10 to 12 hours. Don't offer him any kind of hiding place that would serve as a nest box. Keep showers, affectionate cuddling, and offers of fresh foods to a minimum. Female cockatiels don't get as noisy in this mood as the males, but they're stimulated to lay eggs, and the same treatment shuts that mechanism down as well.

Two or more cockatiels together can be quieter than having just one cockatiel. One cockatiel depends on his humans for all his companionship. A cockatiel with a cockatiel buddy can talk quietly to his friend in soft cockatiel "language" and get some preening attention. To avoid breeding, two males or two females work well. You can keep a male and a female together if you carefully avoid stimulating breeding behavior. Keep their days short and follow the same tips for quieting vocal males.

Ahhhh! It's happening. Now what?

If your cockatiel is screaming, don't play his game. Don't reward him by walking into the room and talking to him. Offer him only your "I'm here" contact call. If you must walk by his cage during a bout of screaming, don't make eye contact — that's a reward. Don't talk to your cockatiel — that's a reward. Turn your back to him and don't face him — any attention is a reward! Get it? Reward positive behavior and don't reward negative behavior.

One time a cockatiel is likely to be noisy is when you're talking on the phone. Cockatiels are flock animals, and they want to do whatever the rest of the flock is doing. The rest of the flock is you, and you're talking. Your cockatiel has no way of knowing that you're talking to another person — though his ears are sharp enough to know if there's a cockatiel on the other end of the line. Your cockatiel will join in the conversation that he thinks you're having with him. You probably don't consider this the ideal way to have a conversation most of the time. You may need to have your phone conversations in a different room from that in which you house your cockatiel or after he goes to bed.

A cockatiel's volume level will match that of the general household. Keep that in mind if you play the TV loudly or your family has loud discussions. Of course, the solution to a loud cockatiel in a loud environment is to lower the volume level. Another potential solution is a slight move. Move your cockatiel's cage away from the TV, away from the speakers, or into another room.

When you come home from work or from an outing, your arrival is a big event for your cockatiel. He may vocalize loudly, as his flock is coming back together and he has the prospect of treats and dinner. If you need to run into the bathroom or do a few chores before you're ready to play with your cockatiel, why not offer him a quieting distraction? Give your cockatiel a treat or some papers to shred or let him play quietly outside his cage on a favorite play gym. A little distraction works wonders, and he'll forget all about his earlier insistence on your immediate attention. Of course, this approach assumes that you eventually have time for your cockatiel and just need a brief respite when you first come home.

A cockatiel who screams at length — make that incessantly — in the middle of the day is annoying. To discourage that behavior, give your cockatiel a timeout, just as you would for a child. Of course, you can't explain what's going on to a cockatiel, so make a timeout brief. Put him in a small cage and darken it with a cover. Leave him in there for five or ten minutes. A timeout isn't meant to be a way of life. A cockatiel won't sit in a darkened cage regretting his transgressions. This disciplinary action is another way of distracting him and getting him to move on to something besides screaming.

If your cockatiel is a screamer, don't neglect a couple of the basics. Be sure that your cockatiel gets enough sleep and enough exercise. If he has clipped wings, take some time to hold his feet and let him "fly" with you. Keep your cockatiel on a sleep schedule by putting him to bed before you watch the late show. A cockatiel who isn't getting enough sleep is crabby, just as a young child would be. He's more likely to nip and may be irritable and noisy.

Biting

Despite what you may think of the weapon a cockatiel has in the form of his beak, it's not natural for a cockatiel to bite with the intent to do harm. A cockatiel's beak is strong and pointed in order to efficiently eat seeded grasses and open dried seeds. Think about it. If cockatiels went around hurting each other in the wild, what would happen to the flock? Cockatiels express frustration and anger with posturing, wing displays, and vocalizations. They limit physical contact with each other to beak wrestling, fake passes at an adversary's feet, or plucking a feather here or there.

In a pinch or in a potentially life-threatening situation, a cockatiel does have a sharp beak and powerful muscles to operate it. What's natural and what happens in our living room are two different things. It would be natural for a cockatiel who encounters a fearful event to stay and fight or to fly away. But we limit a cockatiel's ability to do what comes naturally when we put him in a cage or clip his wings. He can't fly out of the cage to safety. In the choice between fight or flight, he's left only with fight. When a cockatiel can't behave as instinct tells him he should, he replaces his instinctual behavior.

Defining a bite

You can't assume that anytime a cockatiel uses his beak he is reaching out to bite you. He balances himself on two spindly legs. His beak is an exploratory tool and a third steadying appendage in unbalanced situations. It's normal behavior for a cockatiel to reach out with his beak to determine whether a perch is sturdy enough to hold him. One of his perches in your household is your finger, right? He'll do the same thing that he would for any perch. As your finger approaches, maybe even as you're asking him to step up, your cockatiel will reach out with his beak and make sure that you can hold him (see Figure 11-1). That's not a bite. He won't chomp down; he'll simply tap your finger a little. If you get in the habit of assuming this action is a bite and withdraw your finger, you'll have a very confused cockatiel. He may even exhibit some displacement behavior if his natural behavioral traits are thwarted.

Technically, a bite from a cockatiel is an aggressive action that breaks the skin and draws blood. Cockatiels use their beaks for other behaviors that are not bites. Learn to know the difference!

Figure 11-1:
Is this bird about to bite, or is he just reaching for the finger to climb on?

A cockatiel may also use his beak for communication. Yes, he makes a few chirps and whistles! He may beak tussle with you if he wants more preening or things aren't exactly going his way. Usually a beak tussle is accompanied by angry little chirps. He doesn't bite down, he doesn't draw blood, and he doesn't hurt you. A male cockatiel shows off by drumming his beak on a hard surface. This surface isn't often your head, but if it is, that isn't a bite, either.

A cockatiel who is afraid is the most likely to bite. Recognizing what your cockatiel's body language means is helpful in this type of situation. A frightened bird makes himself really big by fluffing out every feather on his body. His eyes will be big, his beak open, and his crest up, and he'll probably be swaying side to side and hissing. A startled cockatiel will be tall and skinny, on the alert, with all his feathers close to his body and his crest straight up. Handling a fearful or cornered cockatiel roughly, or handling him at all in this moment, may result in a bite — a *real* bite. The kind where he chomps down and your blood flows. A really frightened cockatiel chomps down and holds that position, maybe working his beak. It's painful.

Avoiding bites

If you can read your cockatiel's body language and can learn not to push him when he's frightened, you have a good start on understanding how to not get bitten by your cockatiel. In his scared moments, talk to him, reassure him, and handle him gently. Shepherd a scared cockatiel from behind, maneuver him on to a stick, or rescue him and put him back in a secure place. Leave him alone till the fright passes, and then reach down safely and ask him to step up.

Your cockatiel is more likely to bite you if you expect him to bite you. You are in control. Act confident that he will step on your finger, visualize your cockatiel being charming and good, and talk to him in a positive manner. Tell him how much you appreciate his good behavior, beautiful features, and the ways he fills your life with wonder. When your cockatiel is good, tell him so.

Attitude can make a difference in our lives, and when you learn to cultivate a good attitude about your relationship with your cockatiel, the relationship works better. Cockatiels have different key senses than people do or than other pets do. They rely on visual cues and their hearing to tell them how things are going. They probably learn to interpret the cues that people give them, so don't act like you expect to be bitten, and be confident in your interaction with your cockatiel.

If your cockatiel is on your finger or arm and reaches down to bite you (and you're sure that this is a bite, or at least sure that you're being "beaked" harder than you want), you can make your cockatiel reconsider this behavior by shaking your arm. This reaction throws your cockatiel a little off balance. When this has happened a few times, always when your cockatiel intends to bite, he'll get the message.

Stopping biting behavior before it begins

Some factors can influence a cockatiel's tendency to bite. Some cockatiels get very uppity when their wings grow out and they can reach high places and get away from you. If your cockatiel's behavior is changing, check those wings. Maybe it's time to trim them again. A cockatiel can get dramatically better at flying with only one primary feather grown in on each wing.

Your cockatiel will be more defensive, aggressive, and territorial when his hormones are racing. He will be more likely to bite. Cockatiels don't have a breeding season; they're ready to breed anytime that conditions are right. A cockatiel stimulated to be in breeding mode searches for and guards a nesting site, which is probably a dark space such as the inside of a cupboard or drawer or under furniture. Even the bottom of his cage can be a nesting site. Both male and female cockatiels explore for nesting sites, brood eggs, and raise young, so either sex may exhibit this behavior. Other breeding-mode behaviors are lots of vocal activity from males as they show off for a potential mate, and a quickness about willingness to bite.

You can keep hormonal levels to a minimum by giving your companion cockatiel stimuli that are the opposite of what they need to breed. Keep the number of daylight hours your cockatiel is up to 10 to 12 hours. Don't let your cockatiel join you for the late show and cover your cockatiel's cage overnight. The presence of a mate and a nesting spot are other stimuli for breeding, so be your cockatiel's companion, not her mate, and don't let her explore dark places that would make a good nest area. Some types of birds are comforted by roosting in dark places, but not cockatiels. They go into breeding mode.

Another way to avoid being bitten by your cockatiel is to learn what he's saying with his body language and vocalizations. As you learn to recognize body language that says, "I'm going to bite you if you approach me now," then you can wait, talk soothingly, or use a stick instead of your finger for handling your cockatiel. Your cockatiel won't need to bite you as part of his communication repertoire if you establish other ways of communication. Observe your cockatiel closely. When he's asking you to scratch him, move him across the room, or give him your attention, then answer him. Your answer may be no, but a cockatiel who is understood and acknowledged has fewer reasons to bite.

If you have a cockatiel who bites, set strict rules about access to your shoulder. It's not safe to have a biting cockatiel near your face, your lips, your ears, and your eyes. If you know that your cockatiel bites, hold him on your hand and crook your arm so there's no straight highway to your shoulder. Perch him on your knee when seated or put him on a perch or play gym and interact from there. Safety first!

Bonding to One Person

Cockatiels may seem to take a stronger liking to one person in your family than to another. Sometimes this situation is fine, especially if the family members not singled out for the cockatiel's attention don't feel any attraction for your cockatiel. If you're the cockatiel's favorite person, you probably want other members of the family to also play with or care for your cockatiel at times. Ideally, a cockatiel should establish good relationships with all members of a family.

Starting with your behavior

Do you secretly enjoy being the sole object of your cockatiel's affection? If you do, then chances are good that you act out this pleasure over the attention. No matter what you say or negotiate with your family, you project control or affection or are soaking up your cockatiel's love and attention. No one said this behavior was wrong, but you need to recognize what's happening to make changes. Psychological issues may be involved in a family in which a cockatiel is being steered to exhibit behavior that shows he likes someone in the family best. This book focuses on bird behavior modification, but if you find you need a people counselor, then by all means seek one out.

Sharing your cockatiel's affections takes your cooperation. First, identify some daily tasks associated with caring for your cockatiel that involve interaction with a person. Also figure out what rewards are for your cockatiel. What are his favorite treats and favorite rewards?

A reward for a cockatiel may be an edible tidbit. It may also be a verbal "good bird" or a scritch behind his crest or over his ear patches.

To change your cockatiel's behavior, you have to give up some of your cockatiel chores to another person, or even to several members of the family. Basically, you're going to help family members build their own relationships with the family cockatiel. This plan will work even better if you agree that this is a good idea.

Moving on to others' behavior

Your significant other or other members of your family should be assigned to specific interactions with your cockatiel in order to build their own relationship with him. Here are some ways that family members can interact with a cockatiel:

- ✔ Changing cage papers
- ✔ Cooking warm food for the cockatiel
- ✔ Exercising the cockatiel
- ✔ Feeding the cockatiel
- ✔ Giving the cockatiel a snack through cage bars
- ✔ Letting the cockatiel out of his cage
- ✔ Playing with the cockatiel
- ✔ Preening the cockatiel
- ✔ Serving greens and veggies to the cockatiel
- ✔ Showering the cockatiel
- ✔ Showering with the cockatiel
- ✔ Taking the cockatiel to school, work, or a meeting
- ✔ Talking to the cockatiel
- ✔ Spending time with the cockatiel on his playground in another room
- ✔ Trick training the cockatiel
- ✔ Writing, reading, or studying with the cockatiel

Dealing with your cockatiel's behavior

Your cockatiel has work to do. Remember, he's not out to please you. The key to his heart and his trust is getting other family members to do things he enjoys. As he learns to associate different family members with activities he enjoys, he should open up to them. Everyone needs to realize this change won't happen overnight. Your cockatiel bonded to you over time, and bonding to the other members of your flock also will take weeks or months. Of course, over those weeks and months, family members need to consistently play their roles in your cockatiel's care.

Cage-Bound Birds

A cage is a safe place for a cockatiel. If a cockatiel doesn't regularly get out of his cage, he may not want to come out. Or that's what you assume. You leave the door open, and your cockatiel doesn't come out to play. You reach into the cage, and he scuttles away or turns around to bite you. Maybe he even sways and hisses. You would, too, if you were accosted in your own safe place.

This situation usually escalates to the point that a cockatiel's owners don't even try to get him out of the cage after a while. Neither you nor your cockatiel can have any fun this way. Like a toddler heading off to his first day of preschool or a college student leaving home life for dorm life, leaving the cage is a good thing for your cockatiel even though he may be wary of doing so.

Coming out of a cage and climbing to the top is a learned behavior. Maybe your cockatiel never learned to do this. Only young cockatiels with adult guidance learn this behavior. You may need to show him what to do. You can prompt your cockatiel by offering coveted treats along the way. For example, open the cage door and place his morning greens or a small cup of seeds outside the door. After a few days, curiosity should get the better of him, so he'll come out. If he'll follow a treat in your hand, coax him up the side of the cage. You can even put a bird ladder there, making it even easier to get up.

If your have a really reticent cockatiel, capture him in his cage with a towel and take him away from the cage — to neutral territory — to work on his behavior. You'll be amazed at the difference in the bird you're working with. Be sure his wings are clipped. If he's a frightened cockatiel, take him to a small space such as the bathroom or a walk-in closet. Just sit with him for 15 to 20 minutes. Repeat this simple exercise for a few days to a few weeks. Guide him up to your knee to sit, so he knows that you can provide him with a high vantage point. Take it slow.

After your cockatiel will accept some handling, help him learn the Up command (see Chapter 10) to get onto your finger or a stick. You can teach this lesson gradually, perhaps in the evening when everyone is watching TV. Just let your cockatiel be with the family, not demanding anything from him. As he relaxes in this situation, work up to more interaction. Talk to your cockatiel, give him treats of popcorn, rice cracker, or sprigs of parsley. If he flies off his play gym or the back of the couch, go get him, practicing the Up command in a ladder back up to his perch. You're building trust, which is a slow and gradual process. Watch your cockatiel's body carriage and crest placement to figure out when he's comfortable and trusting with each stage of your work.

Feather Plucking

Feather plucking is a complex syndrome. It can indicate either a physical or psychological problem with your cockatiel. You need to observe your bird closely, commit to medical care, and then be creative in solving this issue. This syndrome has many looks. Feather mutilation may range from a bare spot under the wings to a bald chest. It may indicate a deadly disease or could just mean that your cockatiels feel overcrowded in their current accommodations.

Feather plucking is a difficult syndrome for cockatiel owners to face. Much of the beauty and delight of cockatiels is found in their feathers. Underneath it all, a cockatiel looks like a plucked chicken, albeit a plucked chicken with personality! It's worth looking into the reasons for your cockatiel's condition, because feather plucking can be alleviated, or at least controlled, in many cases.

Causes of feather picking

Feather plucking can be caused by disease or allergy. It can be a reaction to toxins or the result of a skin infection. Parasites as well as dietary deficiencies contribute to feather plucking. Some feather plucking is a behavioral response alone, with no medical cause. Because feather plucking has such a range of causes, finding the cause takes some investigation on your part .

Start this investigation with a medical exam by an avian veterinarian. Your vet will want to rule out hypothyroidism, infection, or disease as a cause of the feather picking. Cockatiels commonly have itchy skin and pick only under their wings when they have an infection of the parasite *Giardia*. You or your veterinarian won't know this without lab tests.

Probably one of the worst causes of feather picking is Psittacine Beak and Feather Disease (PBFD). This disease usually affects young birds under 3 years old and causes feathers to grow in abnormally. It's an infectious disease and not curable.

Don't be concerned if your avian veterinarian can't find the cause of your cockatiel's feather picking right away. Work as a team to resolve the problem, as this is such a complex syndrome. Carefully consider the symptoms your bird has and follow your veterinarian's directions regarding ways to rule out different physical causes.

Your cockatiel may be plucking due to sexual frustration. Does your cockatiel pluck feathers at certain times of the year? Is it during the spring and the fall? If this turns out to be the cause, control sexual stimulation or work with your veterinarian to administer hormone shots.

Though it's possible that sexual frustration may be a reason for feather plucking in parrots, breeding your cockatiel isn't the best solution to this problem. If people breed feather-plucking cockatiels, the result in future generations of cockatiels is more feather-plucking cockatiels. Breed only the most outstanding companion cockatiels so that you produce more healthy cockatiels who are well adjusted to life as a human's companion.

Observations about your cockatiel

Your observations about your cockatiel are key to determining his health status. Important observations include details about the age and history of your cockatiel. Where did you get him, and has he lived with other birds and with other species of birds? How long have you observed feather plucking behavior, and when did it start? What does your cockatiel eat? Do you see your cockatiel picking? Is he pulling out feathers, mutilating feathers, or digging sores on his body? Is this a seasonal pattern? Does your cockatiel seem to have itchy skin? How does he react when you see him plucking feathers? Where is your cockatiel plucking? A cockatiel can reach his chest or back. If he's missing feathers from his head, then someone else in the flock is doing the plucking.

Do you or someone in the family smoke or use sprays or chemicals in the home? Have you recently installed new carpeting or started using new scented candles or an air freshener? Is your cockatiel getting a good diet? Does he eat a formulated diet supplemented with fresh foods or a homemade diet and vitamins? Do you feed something other than seed? Does he have access to cuttlebone? Do you have full-spectrum lights in your cockatiel's environment?

Distracting a feather plucker

Whether your cockatiel is plucking feathers for medical or behavioral reasons, you can make several changes that may help your cockatiel feel better about himself and his condition. Bathe your cockatiel daily while his condition persists. Doing so will minimize bacteria and molds as well as irritants to which he is allergic. If your cockatiel is suffering from separation anxiety, his preening following a bath gives him something to do.

Don't give your cockatiel any attention for plucking. Don't admonish him to stop or say no or run over to distract him. Those responses aren't helpful, and your attention may be exactly what he craves. Give your plucking cockatiel attention for playing quietly or for resting peacefully. Tell him how beautiful he is in those moments, as that is behavior you want to encourage.

Offer a plucking cockatiel other outlets for constructive preening. Give him toys that allow him to run his beak over strands of fiber just as he would run his beak through feathers to preen. He can learn to compulsively destroy a toy instead of his own feathers. Let your cockatiel play with peacock feathers or perforate your junk mail. A small whisk-broom or piece of all-cotton rope offer preening opportunities. Change your bird's toys, even if you simply rotate the same toys every other week. If your cockatiel's plucking stems from boredom or if you need to redirect his behavior, rotating the toys is helpful. If your cockatiel is stressed and fearful, however, this tactic probably isn't a good idea.

Part IV
Keeping Cockatiels Healthy

The 5th Wave   By Rich Tennant

"It's 'Feathers', I think she's taking steroids."

In this part . . .

I describe the various toxins and dangers that lurk in your very home, with the aim of helping you to prevent accidents. I also provide advice on first aid and describe warning signs that you should look for if you suspect that your bird is ill.

Chapter 12

Coming to the Rescue

· ·

In This Chapter

▶ Recognizing the signs of illness in a cockatiel

▶ Preparing for injuries, illness, and other emergencies!

▶ Preventing theft of a companion bird

▶ Facing the inevitable

· ·

*O*bserving your cockatiel's daily behavior is a good habit to get into for two reasons: so that you know what's normal for him and so that you can spot the first sign of illness. Your cockatiel relies on you to provide him medical care if things aren't going well. Simple signs may indicate illness. For example, you may notice a change in your bird's routine or fewer droppings on the papers in the cage. Or maybe your normally loquacious bird stops talking and whistling Your cockatiel will probably have a couple illnesses during his 20-year life span. In addition, you can expect your cockatiel to have some accidents because of his curious nature.

You want to be able to make a good judgment about what supportive care to give your cockatiel at home and when to take him to an avian veterinarian. You can be prepared for many emergencies with a first aid kit, and in general, you should be prepared at all times for a disaster such as a fire, tornado, flood, or earthquake. You assume the responsibility for a life when you take on cockatiel ownership. Part of that responsibility is preparing for his care should you pass on. I hope you won't need to refer to this chapter often, but you'll be glad it's here when you need it.

Cockatiels under the Weather

When your cockatiel doesn't feel well, signs may vary from a general depression to obvious misery. Your cockatiel may exhibit a nasal discharge or tail pumping or sit on the bottom of the cage all puffed up. Outwardly, many illnesses have the same or similar symptoms. You need to partner with your avian veterinarian to discover what's wrong.

Here are signs of illness that you should be aware of:

- Tail pumping
- Sitting on both feet
- Puffiness around eyes
- Discharge from nostrils
- Runny or discolored feces (before panicking, consider whether a new food, a diet change, or other major stress could be the culprit)
- Sticky residue on head
- Depression or lethargy
- Cessation of whistling or vocalization
- Feather abnormalities
- Crustiness around beak, eyes, or feet
- Consumption of large quantities of water
- Lowered appetite or fewer droppings
- White plaques inside mouth
- Weight loss

Cockatiels, and in fact all companion birds, hide symptoms of disease. Because they're prey species, in the wild, a sign of weakness would mean they would be somebody's lunch. This makes regular checkups and keen observation of your cockatiel's behavior important clues to their real health status.

First Aid

You're the first line of defense when your cockatiel is ill or injured. He needs your calm head and knowledge of his needs to get through this "first" aid until an avian veterinarian can check him out and administer appropriate care. Here are some basic tips:

- Reduce the chance of further injury by keeping your cockatiel still and quiet.
- Eliminate stress. Put your cockatiel in a dimly lit, quiet place.
- Warmth is important for an ill or injured bird.
- Make sure that food and water are accessible.
- Offer his favorite foods (even if they're birdie "candy").
- Call your avian veterinarian or emergency veterinary clinic.

Keep a first aid kit

If a cockatiel can find a way to get into trouble, he will. His flight instinct will take over, and he'll crash into something, injuring a wing or a leg. In the kitchen, he could fly into boiling water, a sizzling frying pan or an appliance in use. If a non-stick pan overheats, your pal could die in minutes. If you're cooking with chocolate or avocado, your bird could be poisoned. For these emergencies where you're the first recourse, having some first aid items on hand is a good idea. You can buy pre-made avian first aid kits or assemble your own. Remember to use these kits, along with your hospital cage (see the section "Setting up a hospital cage" later in this chapter), to keep your injured cockatiel comfortable until you can get the professional help of an avian veterinarian.

A basic cockatiel first aid kit should contain the following:

- **Styptic powder:** Apply this to bleeding feathers or nails to stop the bleeding, but do not apply to open wounds. Look for ferric subsulfate powder (styptic powder) available commercially. A popular brand is called Kwik Stop. Pack the powder into a bleeding nail, but don't use it to stop bleeding from wounds on a bird's body and don't use it in a bird's mouth. If you don't have styptic powder, you can use cornstarch or flour, or you can be press a bleeding nail into a bar of soap.

- **Vet wrap:** Vet wrap sticks to itself and can be used to restrain a cockatiel's wings so he doesn't do further damage to himself. You could also make a hasty splint from vet wrap for a broken leg.

- **Towel:** Use for restraint, but remember not to compress your cockatiel's chest when restraining him.

- **Eyewash solution:** Eyewash is a saline solution and can be used to rinse out wounds. If it's not available, use warm water. When your cockatiel is wounded, your first task is to clean the wound. Don't use any kind of ointment on the cockatiel's wound, and get him to the veterinarian as soon as possible, who can administer medical care.

- **Syringe:** Use it to flush wounds or to hand-feed an ill bird.

- **Cotton swabs:** Use to clean wounds.

- **Hemostat or tweezers:** Use these to firmly grip a broken blood feather that is bleeding profusely. Hemostats are pointed scissors that lock in place so they have a good grip.

- **Plastic bag:** Save any substance and its container if your cockatiel has eaten something that is poisonous. Bring along leaves of a plant that may be poisonous.

A cockatiel first aid kit can be handy in several places. Take one along if you board your cockatiel, or make one accessible to your pet sitter. Be sure that you include one among your emergency supplies. If you travel, take one with you. If you're a pet sitter or provide foster care for cockatiels, keep one in your home and one in your car. Your avian veterinarian may be able to help you locate some of the supplies.

Don't use any kind of ointment on your bird as a part of your first aid. Use only a saline solution to thoroughly clean a wound. A bird could spread oil from an ointment to his feathers and would then lose his ability to keep himself warm — just when he needs it the most.

Be prepared

Think about and prepare for an emergency that could force you to evacuate your home. In the event of a fire, flood, chemical spill, earthquake, or tornado, you need to leave your home quickly, taking your cockatiel with you. How will you get your cockatiel out of the house, what will he have to eat, and how will you identify your cockatiel if you must leave him at a shelter for a period of time?

Here are some tips to help you prepare for the possibility of disaster:

- ✔ Have a carrier to get your cockatiel out of the house.

- ✔ Know where the carrier is located.

- ✔ If you have more than one bird, do a mental triage of your animals. If you can only save one (the fire is roaring, the water is rising) which would it be? Only two of the three? As a last resort, you can free flighted birds from their cages to fend for themselves.

If you don't have enough carriers to quickly get your birds out of the house, you can use a pillowcase, an empty purse, or a shoe box.

If you're as proud of your cockatiel as most owners are, snap his picture at some point. Keep that picture and veterinary records in a plastic bag with your other important papers. If you do have time to grab those papers before you leave your house, your record of ownership, a list of medications the bird requires, and a picture for a "lost bird" poster are all at hand. Another good idea is to include a list of your cockatiel's preferences and idiosyncrasies. Write down the food he eats, his favorite treats, words he knows, and tunes he can whistle. If you need to turn him over to someone for temporary care, you have the instruction manual ready.

Find out whether your county or state has an emergency plan for animals. Some use fairgrounds or shelters as places for people and their pets in the event of an emergency. Many emergency shelters for people do not accept their animals.

The primary supplies to have on hand in case of emergency are bird food and clean water. Always be prepared. Get more food when you're down to half a carton or bag. Store drinking water and rotate your supply as you use it.

Your cockatiel is used to eating from dishes, but in an emergency, paper plates, a napkin, a clean ashtray, or your dog's bowl can be put into service. You know better than anyone how messy a bird can be. As part of emergency supplies, keep trash bags handy so that you can clean up after your own pet.

Setting up a hospital cage

One of the best, most nurturing things you can do for your bird when he's ill or injured is to keep him warm and comfortable until you can see an avian veterinarian. One way to do this is to turn the cockatiel's cage into a *hospital cage* for your feathered friend. Preparing a hospital cage is easy. Start by making food and water easily accessible. Put the food and water on the floor of the cage, especially if your cockatiel isn't feeling well enough to perch. Keep your bird in a darkened and warm environment. You can create a low-light situation by keeping the bird in a darkened, quiet room or by wrapping the cage in towels. A light bulb or heating pad can supply warmth. Be sure that your bird also has an area of the cage where he can get away from the heat source and adjust his own comfort level.

Instead of a cage, you can use a corrugated box or a fish tank, or you can even invest in a brooder, which is a device meant to hold a steady temperature to keep unfeathered parrot chicks warm. Brooders give young birds the same environment an older, but ill, bird needs: dark, quiet, and warmth. Watch your bird for signs that he's too hot or too cold. If he's too hot, he'll pant, slick down his feathers, and hold his wings out to the side. If he's too cold, he'll fluff up to take advantage of his natural down coat, sit on his feet to keep them warm, and shiver. If he's just right (this is beginning to sound like a story we all know), he'll perch naturally with his feathers neither puffed out nor slicked to his body.

Preventing Theft

Cockatiels are not expensive, desirable birds prone to theft. If you have a particularly fun whistler or chatty cockatiel, though, everyone in the neighborhood may know he's there, so someone may want him. If your interest in birds has grown and you also have even more valuable parrots in your home now, security is a concern.

Whenever you're out with your cockatiel or other birds, don't divulge your home address (give out a P.O. box or a voice mail box as contact information).

Outdoor protections

You can design your landscaping to provide security. Be sure that walkways are well lit by using motion sensor lights or other lighting. Plant thorny bushes such as roses under ground-floor windows, making them less than desirable entry points. If you own a dog, he can serve as a good warning system. Bird aviaries or bird rooms that aren't attached to a house should be able to be secured, with all the birds roosting inside a locked building. Consider installing a sound or video monitor if you're concerned about security.

Vacation preparation

It's really good news that you can take time for a relaxing vacation. Don't advertise it to the neighborhood, however. One benefit of having a pet sitter come to your home is that he can keep a house looking lived in by turning the lights on and off pulling the shades up and down. If a pet sitter or house sitter is not coming to your house, maybe a relative or friend can move your cars in and out of the garage occasionally. Have someone take out your garbage on trash pickup day, and make sure that your grass is mowed or your walks shoveled of snow. Put your lights on timers so that they go on and off appropriately, and arrange for a radio to play for that "lived-in" feel to your home. By all means stop home delivery of the newspaper and ask the post office to hold your mail so that neither piles up while you're gone.

Preparing for the End

Cockatiels are long-lived animal companions, but they don't live forever. They're also prone to diseases that could shorten their expected life span, just as people are. Our lives are precious, and our only certainty is that we are here, now. Think about what will happen to the feathered being for which you're responsible if today is the only day you are here, or if that day comes much sooner than you expect.

For anyone who has not experienced the companionship of a cockatiel, describing the bond that develops between a person and their bird is difficult. Realize that you will grieve the passing of your companion cockatiel, and that's normal. Your friends without pet birds may not be sympathetic, but online groups, pet loss experts, and support groups can help you cope. Your local animal shelter can probably help you find these groups.

Scenario: Your cockatiel dies before you do

I recommend that you have a necropsy, which is the word for a bird's autopsy, performed when your cockatiel dies. A necropsy is a good idea for several reasons. Doing a necropsy can help an avian veterinarian pinpoint the cause of death. If there was an internal problem that did not show up on tests, this procedure either helps to confirm a diagnosis or can alleviate guilt on your part. You can't do anything about a cockatiel who got cancer or had a genetic disease.

If the reason for the cockatiel's death was related to the cleanliness and diet of your cockatiel, then you will have learned more about good care for your remaining birds or your next bird. If you find out that you can't supply the proper environment for a bird, then don't get another one.

If your cockatiel's death was caused by one of the major viral diseases, find out more about the specific disease. Many of these diseases remain in the environment for months or years. You may need to test your remaining birds and do a significant cleanup. If you have no other birds but plan to get one, be sure that you don't expose a new cockatiel to a deadly virus.

Scenario: You're the first to go

As your friends and family meet your cockatiel, you'll discover that he has human friends among them. Get a commitment from one or two (one could be a backup in case circumstances change for the first choice) that they would take your cockatiel if anything ever happens to you. You can ask this favor informally and should also tell close family members of your wishes. If you want to be sure that your wishes are carried out, include instructions for the care of your cockatiel in a will or a trust. The most complete way to care for your cockatiel and other pets when you die is to create a trust for them. The trustee you specify will then receive the pet or pets and money to care for them over the course of their natural lives. Of course, these are legal matters, and laws vary by state. Consult a legal professional about an appropriate course of action.

If you don't feel that any of your friends or family are appropriate caretakers of your cockatiel, look for a nearby parrot adoption center, which will try to place your cockatiel in its next cockatiel-loving home. Adoption centers have expenses to meet and appreciate a bequest to cover your bird's care until he can be placed. You may even commit to a monthly donation to the center of your choice. Adoption centers are sometimes run by bird clubs or may be run by private individuals. Here are a few of the major adoption centers; you can possibly get a referral to an agency near you.

✔ Mickaboo Cockatiel Rescue: PO Box 1631 Pacifica, CA 94044; phone: 650-870-1421 and 650-870-1421; e-mail mail@mickaboo.org; Web site www.mickaboo.org

✔ Parrot Education and Adoption Center (PEAC): PO Box 600423, San Diego CA 92160-0423; phone: 619-287-8200; e-mail: parroted@peac.org; www.peac.org

✔ The Gabriel Foundation: PO Box 11477, Aspen, CO 81612; phone: 970-963-2620; e-mail: gabriel@thegabrielfoundation.org; Web site www.thegabrielfoundation.org/

Sanctuaries are also available to care for companion birds. A sanctuary commits to lifetime care of the companion birds they take in. However, your cockatiel, as a beloved pet, would be better off with another cockatiel-loving person or family rather than at a sanctuary.

Here's a good idea for not only cockatiel owners but owners of any types of pets: Carry a card in your wallet that says you care for animals at home. You never know when you may be incapacitated or involved in an accident. On your card list an emergency contact who should be notified that your cockatiel needs care. If you are so inclined, list your companion animals and their veterinarians as well. A couple forward-thinking bird clubs put out such cards — what a great idea to give you extra peace of mind. If you don't have a pre-printed emergency contact card, write the necessary information on a slip of paper that you keep in your wallet and update it from time to time.

With all of the eventualities taken care of, I wish you and your cockatiel a long and happy life! May your plans for disaster and death give you peace of mind, but go unused. May you and your cockatiel age gracefully together in an active old age.

Chapter 13

Lifelong Health Care

. . . .

. . . .

*Y*ou expect your avian veterinarian to thoroughly understand the major diseases and conditions that affect captive cockatiels. But it's also helpful for you to know something about them so that you can recognize health problems in their early stages, enabling your veterinarian to start appropriate treatment as soon as possible. Some diseases are commonly diagnosed and treatable. Avian medicine is making rapid progress, so rely on your own reading of current periodicals and the latest advice from your veterinarian to treat your cockatiel. Alternative medicine is increasingly popular in both human and companion animal medicine, so be on the lookout for ways to treat your cockatiel with acupuncture, touch, herbs, and homeopathic remedies.

The very best medicine for your cockatiel is prevention. Minimize exposure to pathogens. Don't take your cockatiel to bird club meetings, pet shops, or bird fairs where she could be exposed to many birds from many aviaries.

Keep your cockatiel well fed with a varied, nutritious diet. Keep her cage clean and keep her mind active. In turn, she'll be able to fight infection and continue her job of being a fine companion for you.

Common Cockatiel Conditions

Your cockatiel, even if she looks and acts great, may have one of the commonly diagnosed cockatiel infections. Remember that cockatiels mask illness and that lab tests are essential. The good news is that most common cockatiel illnesses are treatable. A cockatiel on a good diet and in exceptional health will fight off most illnesses; a cockatiel with an undiagnosed ailment, malnutrition, or constant stress may have chronic infections.

Bacterial infections

Bacterial infections, which are caused by microorganisms, seem to be fairly common in cockatiels. A lab test is required to accurately diagnose infections because the microorganisms involved can't be seen with the naked eye. The normal bacterial flora of a cockatiel are gram-positive, as determined by a gram stain lab test. Your veterinarian may tell you that tests indicate your cockatiel has a gram-negative bacterial infection and should be treated with antibiotics. Mild infections usually don't require treatment; your veterinarian will make that decision.

A cockatiel's normal bacterial flora is gram-positive, and a person's bacterial flora is gram-negative. The bacteria in human saliva are not healthy for a cockatiel. Don't let your cockatiel take food from your mouth, clean your teeth, or bite into anything you have tasted first. No kisses for your cockatiel!

To a careful observer, some signs may signal an infection in your bird. However, sometimes your bird will show no signs at all. This is yet another reason that regular veterinary exams are so important. Signs of a bacterial infection include listlessness, gaping (see Chapter 9), and a change in behavior.

Yeast infection

A common infection in cockatiels is *candidiasis,* or a yeast infection. In people, we call a similar infection *thrush.* This infection usually involves the digestive tract, including the mouth, crop, and throat, but may extend to the intestines. A yeast infection is caused by an overgrowth of the common fungus *Candida albicans.* Even healthy birds have some *C. albicans* in their systems, but an overgrowth of the fungus occasionally occurs.

Signs of a yeast infection include the presence of white, cheesy lesions in the mouth, weight loss, thickened crop, frequent regurgitation, diarrhea, and sudden death (not common). In some cases, your bird may not exhibit any symptoms that she has a yeast infection. The success of yeast infection treatment depends on how soon the condition is diagnosed and the general health of the bird.

Here are some situations in which cockatiels are more likely to get a yeast infection:

- ✔ In chicks, which have less highly developed immune systems
- ✔ In any bird after antibiotic therapy

 ✔ When the bird's diet is deficient in vitamin A

 ✔ When a bird is fed moldy food (especially sprouts)

 ✔ In poor sanitary conditions, which increase exposure to the fungus

If your cockatiel is treated with antibiotics, ask your veterinarian about treatment at the same time to prevent a yeast infection.

Adding apple cider vinegar to your cockatiel's drinking water helps to acidify its system so that yeast does not grow. Add a tablespoon of vinegar to 8 ounces of water, and supply it as the drinking water for a week or two at a time.

Giardia

Giardia is a parasite that can infect dogs, cats, horses, and humans as well as birds. As far as the medical experts can determine, however, infected birds can't pass on an infection to people or other mammals. The birds most often infected with giardia are cockatiels, budgies, lovebirds, and grey-cheeked parakeets.

Cockatiels get giardia from ingesting cysts found in contaminated food or water. The cysts produce trophozoites, which attach themselves to the lining of the bird's intestine and produce more cysts. These cysts are excreted in the feces, and the cycle goes on. Cysts are resistant to drying, boiling, and freezing, though some disinfectants are effective against them. Thoroughly cleaning your cockatiel's cage and environment should be part of the treatment for giardia.

Giardia can affect a cockatiel's ability to absorb some nutrients. In cockatiels especially, it can also lead to severe itching. Giardia in birds seems to be a regional problem and can be difficult to cure, although it can be treated. Cockatiels with giardiasis may have no symptoms or may have one or more of the following symptoms:

 ✔ Whole seeds in droppings

 ✔ Partially digested food in droppings

 ✔ Dry, flaky skin

 ✔ Patchy feather loss

 ✔ Shifting leg lameness

 ✔ Persistent feather picking (especially wings, flanks, and legs)

 ✔ Recurrent yeast infections

 ✔ Lethargy

 ✔ Loss of appetite

 ✔ Weight loss

 ✔ Diarrhea

 ✔ Messiness, lack of preening

 ✔ Itching

 ✔ Wasting of the breast muscles

 ✔ Yellow urates (the white part of a normal dropping)

 ✔ No response to antibiotic therapy when bacterial infection is suspected

Pesky P Diseases

For some reason, a high percentage of the major bird diseases start with the letter *p*. Pretty peculiar! I list them here, with their major symptoms. A cockatiel may get any of them or have none of them. Even good breeders and pet stores may occasionally have disease in their flock. They work with a veterinarian to control and/or eliminate it, and they're honest about the presence of disease, passing on information to you that may affect the health status of your cockatiel.

Psittacosis

Psittacosis, which is also called chlamydiosis, is caused by a bacteria called *Chlamydia psittaci*. Cockatiels tolerate psittacosis especially well, meaning that they may have the disease or infect other birds without showing outward signs of the infections themselves. Signs of psittacosis include watery yellow or lime green droppings, loss of appetite, depression, listlessness, nasal discharges, and sudden death (not common). Cockatiels are often accused of infecting other birds, and many parrot breeders are wary of also keeping cockatiels. Psittacosis is usually treatable.

This is one of the *zoonotic diseases,* or diseases that can be transmitted to people by animals. The disease is spread when infected birds shed the *Chlamydia* organism in respiratory discharges, droppings, and feather dust, as well as through contaminated food and water. People who contract psittacosis usually experience flulike symptoms, including pounding headaches and weakness, and can experience respiratory problems or even get pneumonia, requiring hospitalization.

If your cockatiel is kept around people with suppressed immune systems, she should have routine veterinary exams to rule out psittacosis. It is important to quarantine newly acquired birds. Ask your veterinarian about new developments in psittacosis diagnosis, treatment, and prevention.

Polyomavirus

This virus, which normally affects young birds just as they wean, is usually transmitted by adult carriers. The disease results in the sudden death of what appears to be a healthy young bird. Birds often have abdominal enlargement and bleeding underneath the skin. Signs of polyomavirus include delayed crop emptying, weakness, appetite loss, abdominal enlargement, bleeding under the skin, tremors, paralysis, diarrhea, regurgitation, feather abnormalities (sometimes), and sudden death.

A test and a vaccine are available for this virus, but there is no treatment for a bird with the disease.

Psittacine beak and feather disease

This highly contagious disease, often known simply as PBFD, primarily affects young birds. It may be spread by ingesting contaminated feather dust or droppings. The virus is long lived outside the body and resistant to many common disinfectants. PBFD can be diagnosed with a blood test. Signs of PBFD include depression, diarrhea, crop problems, abnormal feathers, loss of normal powder on feathers, and beak lesions.

If a cockatiel does contract PBFD, it is fatal. Work is being done to develop a vaccine to prevent this disease. Check with your avian veterinarian about the status of the research.

Pacheco's disease virus

Pacheco's disease virus (PDV) is induced by a herpes virus. It may last a few days or a few weeks but is most often rapidly fatal. In many species this disease is 100 percent fatal, though a survival rate of 20 percent has been reported in cockatiels. These hardy little birds triumph once again.

Signs of Pacheco's disease virus include regurgitation, lethargy, increased thirst, diarrhea, orange-colored urates, and sudden death. The disease affects the liver, spleen, and kidneys. Many outbreaks are linked to a stressful event, such as environmental changes or breeding. A vaccine is available for this virus, though it is controversial and mainly used by high-risk businesses, such as pet shops.

Proventricular dilatation disease (PDD)

This disease, which affects the digestive tract, was originally called macaw wasting disease, but it affects many species of parrots. The proventriculus is a bird's stomach, producing gastric juices that digest food. A cockatiel with PDD cannot digest food and eventually dies from the syndrome. Signs of PDD include depression, weight loss, regurgitation, and/or passage of undigested seeds in the droppings. Central nervous system signs associated with PDD, which may occur in addition to the signs involved in digestion, include abnormal head movements, seizures, and lack of mobility.

When this book was written, researchers at the University of Georgia were working on identifying the pathogen involved so that a test for it could be developed and preventive measures could be identified. Major progress continues in avian medical research, mainly because of the support of companion bird owners.

One of the major fundraisers for PDD research has been "The Grey PoopOn Challenge" with its online fund raisers and conferences. For more information, contact: TGPC, PMB 293, 5694 Mission Center Rd., Ste. 602, San Diego CA 92108-9715; Web site `http://members.tripod.com/Grey_PoopOn/`.

Other Diseases

Okay, not all cockatiel diseases start with the letter *p*. Some of them start with other letters.

Aspergillosis

Aspergillosis is a fungal disease of the sinuses, lungs, or air sacs. It is caused by the *fungus Aspergillus fumigatus*. This fungus is everywhere in the environment, and both birds and people are constantly exposed to it. It is found in soil, rotted wood, corncob bedding, aviary dust, and stored seeds and grains.

Birds with compromised immune systems are most likely to get an aspergillus infection. Low humidity, high humidity without ventilation, or high air dust in the environment also contributes to aspergillosis. Signs of aspergillosis include wheezing, respiratory clicking, voice changes, increased breathing rate, weight loss, increased urination, and death.

The only symptom may be sudden death, or a bird may have respiratory problems signaling this disease. Diagnosis is difficult, except through necropsy. Reducing stress and providing a clean environment are essential in preventing infection. Though some treatments are available, aspergillosis often results in death.

Tuberculosis (TB)

In birds, tuberculosis is caused by *Mycobacterium avium, M. tuberculosis* (the TB agent that affects humans), or other TB mycobactyerium species. TB can be transmitted through food or water, contaminated perches, or cage wire. Ticks, mites, and spiders can transmit the disease to birds, as well. A cockatiel also can contact TB through a skin wound that the bird comes in contact with through contaminated objects.

In cockatiels, TB is typically a disease of the digestive system. (This is in contrast to human beings, in which TB is usually a disease of the respiratory system.) Tuberculosis is a chronic infection in which lesions called tubercles form. These lesions can be found in the bird's intestinal wall, liver, spleen, and bone marrow and often appear on the skin. At first the lesions are soft, but they harden over time.

Birds exhibit few outward symptoms of this disease, and the symptoms that do appear could be characteristic of many problems. Signs of avian TB include weight loss, masses under the skin, thinness despite a good appetite, recurrent diarrhea, intermittent lameness, breathing problems, swollen joints, bright red blood in droppings, cloacal prolapse (when a cockatiel's insides are coming out through his vent, looking like a red cherry on his bottom), lethargy and depression, and abdominal enlargement.

TB can be treated in birds, though the caretaker faces a health risk. In some cases, euthanasia of the cockatiel may be warranted because avian TB can be transmitted to humans, and treating people for the disease is difficult. It is rare for people to contract avian TB, but people with low resistance to disease are at risk, including old and young people, those with serious illnesses such as cancer that lower their resistance to infection, and people with illnesses that compromise the immune system, such as AIDS.

If you have a cockatiel that tests positive for TB, discuss all treatment options with both your veterinarian and your personal physician.

Gout

Gout in cockatiels is the accumulation of uric acid in different sites within the body. There are two types of gout in companion birds:

- ✔ Arterial gout affects the joints of the lower legs and is prevalent in budgies, or parakeets as they are commonly called. The bird becomes lame and develops swellings on its legs. Eventually it is crippled.
- ✔ Visceral gout affects the internal organs of a bird and is difficult to diagnose.

The uric acid deposits typical of either form of gout are caused the inability of the bird's kidneys to remove waste products from the bloodstream. There may be a genetic predisposition to this disease. Cockatiels with this disease are usually put on a special diet by their avian veterinarian.

Alternative Treatments

Birds, along with people and other companion animals, are benefiting from an increased awareness of holistic care by the traditional medical community. The holistic approach to care treats a being's emotional and physical needs. Holistic care giver also feels that it is the body that heals, not the person administering care. The least invasive methods of treatment are administered in holistic care.

A seriously ill bird first needs the intervention of traditional medicine. You may want to supplement traditional treatments with alternative therapies to treat the whole bird. Alternative medicine also may be the right treatment for chronic pain, behavioral issues, or conditions not corrected by traditional veterinary medicine.

Acupuncture

This treatment should be performed by a certified acupuncturist or a veterinarian. Points on a bird's body are stimulated in this treatment by using acupuncture needles, injections, low-level lasers, or magnets. If you choose this course of treatment, you should be with your cockatiel to provide moral support when the therapy is administered. It is believed that birds are more responsive to acupuncture than mammals because of their higher metabolism. A bird's natural inclination may be to pull acupuncture needles from its body instead of letting them remain in position. In that case, the needles may be inserted for only seconds, or vitamin B12 may be injected into the acupuncture points.

Herbal therapy

Both herbs and nutritional therapy are effective in treating disease. Doses for birds have not been developed, however. Herbal therapies are available that are antibacterial, antifungal, and antiviral. Others boost the immune system. Follow the direction of your holistic veterinarian when using herbal therapies.

Though herbs are "natural," they can also be harmful. Don't experiment with them yourself (except when cooking with herbs in your next stew!). Work with your holistic veterinarian about which herbs to use and in what doses.

Homeopathy

Homeopathy is a kind of health care that is more popular throughout the world than Western medicine. In homeopathy, patients are treated with diluted amounts of medicines that would create the same symptoms as the disease if they were given the medicines in larger amounts. Homeopathic remedies help the body heal itself and don't work immediately, but over days and weeks.

Massage

Many companion animals benefit from touch therapy developed by Linda Tellington-Jones and called TTouch by its practitioners. Gentle touches and movement exercises help animals by relieving pain and can be an aid in changing problem behaviors. To find a practitioner, become a practitioner, or subscribe to their newsletter, contact the originators of this therapy: TTEAM/TTouch in USA, P.O. Box 3793, Santa Fe, NM 87501; phone 800-854-8326; Web site http://lindatellingtonjones.com/. You also can find out about this therapy at the ParrotTouch Web site, www.home. earthlink.net/~parrottouch/.

Holistic veterinarians

Here are some sources if you want to find a holistic veterinarian:

- ✔ Natural Holistic Pet Care - Larry A. Bernstein, VMD, 751 N.E. 168 Street, N. Miami Beach, FL 33162-2427 USA; phone: 305-652-5372; fax: 305-653-7244; Web site www.naturalholistic.com

- ✔ The Academy of Veterinary Homeopathy, 6400 East Independence Blvd., Charlotte, NC 28212; phone: 305-652-1590; Web site www.theavh.org/

- ✔ American Holistic Veterinary Medical Association, 2218 Old Emmorton Road, Bel Air, MD 21015; phone: 410-569-0795; e-mail AHVMA@compuserve.com; Web site www.altvetmed.com/ahvmadir.html

- ✔ The American Academy of Veterinary Acupuncture, Box 419, Hygiene, CO 80533-0419; phone 303-772-6726; e-mail AAVAoffice@aol.com; Web site www.aava.org/

Part V
The Part of Tens

The 5th Wave   By Rich Tennant

"He loves his ball and string, but once in a while he'll pick up the trombone and play 'Under Paris Skies' over and over again."

In this part . . .

I give you some fun top-ten lists. I offer you ten mistakes that can spoil cockatiel ownership and ten New Year's resolutions for having the best relationship with your cockatiel.

Chapter 14

Ten Mistakes That Spoil Cockatiel Ownership

In This Chapter

▶ Knowing what you're getting into

▶ Thinking before getting your cockatiel companion a mate

Cockatiels can be loving companions and true members of the family. There's a lot that can go wrong between people and their cockatiels, too. In this chapter, I look at some of the common mistakes that people make when sharing their lives with cockatiels. As human beings, the best thing you can do when you make a mistake is to learn from it. If you can learn from mistakes made by people before you, so much the better! If you see yourself here, know that these experiences happen to real people.

Not educating yourself before acquiring a companion cockatiel: The operative word in this error is "before." Cockatiels require different care than many other companion pets. The time to start reading about them is the moment you decide you'd like a cockatiel, before actually buying or adopting one. If their care requirements mesh with your lifestyle, housing, and current pets, then you can decide it's a go! If having a companion cockatiel really doesn't work for you, consider caring for someone else's cockatiel occasionally, helping a pet shop hand-train its birds, or volunteering for a bird adoption or humane society.

Getting a mate for a companion cockatiel: We can't neuter our cockatiel companions, and they display a desire a desire to breed as well as tangible evidence of the capability, like laying eggs. A companion cockatiel doesn't need a mate when she shows the first sign of interest in breeding Your pet very possibly thinks that you are her mate and would ignore another cockatiel. People don't run out and get mates for their adolescent children when they show interest in the opposite sex. Accept sexuality as part of your bird.

Feeling sorry for an abused cockatiel: After you know something about cockatiel care, you may be tempted to "rescue" cockatiels from breeders or pet stores where you feel their care is less than ideal. Unfortunately, economically supporting a business giving marginal care perpetuates its existence. Think about what you're doing, and buy from adoption centers, breeders, and pet stores with the highest standards. You support them by spending your dollars there.

Stealing eggs from your hen cockatiel: A cockatiel goes through a whole series of hormonal changes when she lays an egg. Her instinct tells her to procreate and raise more cockatiels. When you take her eggs, she may stay in the egg-laying mode, vainly trying to achieve a clutch of four to five eggs to incubate and hatch. It's easier to stop breeding behavior if you allow your female to sit on a clutch of eggs for about a week before taking them away from her. Remember, the type of nest a cockatiel is looking for is a dark, enclosed space.

Cohabiting with predatory animals: Having dogs, birds, and cats together in one household requires proper introductions and monitoring of behavior. Don't ever trust a dog or cat alone with your companion bird. Don't subject your bird to the stress of constantly being hunted.

Assuming this little old cage is big enough: You'll be doing a great kindness to your cockatiel if you house it in the largest cage you can afford and fit in your house. Start saving your pennies.

Thinking it's not any harder to take care of ten cockatiels: You'll probably find it easy to think of reasons to want more cockatiels: Cockatiels each have their own personality. They come in many beautiful colors. A cockatiel needs a home. Someone knows that you have cockatiels and would take good care of the one they no longer want. Realistically, however, you're limited by your time and resources.

Making seeds the main course: Your cockatiel's steady diet should be a formulated diet containing good nutrition in every bite. Seeds lack some amino acids and calcium. Besides, they're high in fat. Just like you eat ice cream or a candy bar only occasionally, seeds should be only an occasional treat for your cockatiel.

Assuming cost = value of a cockatiel: When you take your cockatiel to see an avian veterinarian or consider calling a parrot behaviorist, don't limit his treatment to the cost of your cockatiel when you purchased it. Your bird's medical or behavioral care should reflect your commitment to the cockatiel as a being and as your treasured companion. Don't be too stingy when determining how much veterinary care you can afford. Yes, your first veterinary exam will probably cost more than you paid for your cockatiel! It won't cost thousands of dollars, either. Talk about your options with your veterinarian to reach a happy medium between care level and what you can afford.

Buying a cockatiel for your child: By the time a child is 10 or 11 years old, he may be able to take responsibility for the care of a bird, especially if he likes animals and has been reading and learning about cockatiels. For younger children, however, you will be the primary caretaker. Exposing a household cockatiel to children under 7 years old on a regular basis isn't appropriate. Birds just don't understand their quick movements and erratic behavior. And young children can't tell when they're squeezing too hard as they show a bird some affection.

Chapter 15

Ten New Year's Resolutions

● ●

In This Chapter

▶ Prepare good meals for your bird

▶ Remember that cleanliness comes first

▶ See a veterinarian

▶ Redecorate your cockatiel's cage

▶ Keep on learning

● ●

*E*ven if you're an educated owner, your cockatiel has the best chance of care if you continually learn about birds in general and cockatiels in particular. The more people you meet who have cockatiels, the more ideas you'll get about providing a stimulating life for your cockatiels. It never hurts to review the basics occasionally, either. Start with the reasons you enjoy your cockatiel. Move on to how you can provide your bird's basic requirements in a way that works for you. The next time you make New Year's resolutions or Cockatiel Year's resolutions, or simply take time to review the care of your cockatiel, feel free to adopt these resolutions.

Feed my cockatiel wisely: I'll base my cockatiel's diet on a formulated diet. I'll offer her fresh vegetables and whole grains as snacks. High-calorie foods and seeds will be only occasional treats fed in small amounts. My cockatiel's water bowl will be so clean that I'd be willing to drink out of it!

Keep the cage clean: Knowing that a messy cage can allow the growth of bacteria and molds that are harmful to my cockatiel, I will keep it clean. That means changing papers daily and scrubbing the cage down on a weekly basis. It's easier to keep up with small messes. I'll use a scratchy pad to scrub the cage's grate daily if need be. Of course, I'll keep a vacuum cleaner nearby at all times! I'll scrub the walls, too. I'll even do windows.

Disinfect my cockatiel's enclosure and bowls: At least once a month, I will disinfect my cockatiel's bowls in a bleach solution or other disinfectant. I'll mix ¾ cup bleach in a gallon of water to make a bleach solution. Bowls will soak in this solution for 15 minutes. I'll wipe down the cage with a similar solution, rinse it, and then let it dry. I'll be careful when using disinfectant by allowing plenty of ventilation, removing the bird from the cage, and wearing gloves to protect my hands.

Bathe my cockatiel regularly: We're going to start a new routine, with my cockatiel welcome in the shower with me daily. The misty environment is good for her feathers. On warm days I'll spray my cockatiels once or even several times a day. My reward will be a cockatiel who preens herself into shiny beauty.

Schedule an appointment with an avian veterinarian: My cockatiel should see an avian veterinarian on a regular basis. If it's been a year since the last well-bird check, then it's time for one again. If I've never had an appointment with a veterinarian, it's past time! Once my cockatiel has an emergency, it's too late. I want to have an idea of my cockatiel's weight and health now, for reference. I'll also establish a working relationship with my veterinarian before I need one in an emergency.

Minimize breeding stimuli: This year, I'll use what I know about the cockatiel breeding cycle to minimize stimuli for breeding behavior. I won't let my cockatiel play in dark, enclosed places such as boxes and cupboards. I'll limit her waking hours in a day to 12 or even 10 hours. If that means she needs a "sleeping cage" in a quiet room, I'll provide that. I'll build a bond with her without becoming her surrogate mate. If I fail in all my attempts to stem egg laying, chewing, or aggressive behavior associated with breeding behavior, I'll supply my bird with the supplemental calcium she needs to lay eggs and will be understanding till the mood passes!

Get a night light and day light: This year, I'll supply my cockatiel with her appropriate lighting requirements. I'll get her full-spectrum lighting for the daytime. To prevent night thrashing, I'll make sure that a night light shines near her cage overnight.

Chop more veggies: I'll be adventurous in my choice of vegetables and in their presentation to my cockatiel. I'll buy kale, and I'll mash sweet potatoes. I'll julienne, slice, quarter, shred, cook, mash, and grate carrots. I'll give purple cabbage a try and will feed my cockatiel broccoli even if I don't like it. I may even put more veggies into my own diet at the same time.

Rearrange the furniture for the cockatiel: Maybe I'll move the couch out farther from the wall or move those two chairs closer to the fireplace. Just kidding. When I pledge to rearrange the furniture, I just mean that several times this year, I will redecorate my cockatiel's cage, perhaps by adding fresh branches for perches. At the same time, I'll hang new toys or bring out old toys that my cockatiel hasn't seen in a while and is therefore stimulated to play with anew.

Attend a conference or bird club meeting: This year, I'll take the opportunity to learn more about cockatiels by attending a bird club meeting, joining a bird club, or attending a seminar about companion birds. I'll meet new people, ask questions, and make the experience worthwhile to both my cockatiel and myself. If I'm bursting with information after a few seminars, I'll consider sharing with my own community. I'll look into offering classes at a local pet shop, humane society, recreation facility, or continuing education program. If I don't offer classes, I'll share my cockatiel and my knowledge with a neighbor, a group of schoolchildren, or a group of senior adults. I'll be open to learning from these people and sharing my experiences.

Index

~~SS,~~ CAREERS & PERSONAL FINANCE

0-7645-5307-0

0-7645-5331-3 *†

Also available:

- ✔Accounting For Dummies †
  0-7645-5314-3
- ✔Business Plans Kit For Dummies †
  0-7645-5365-8
- ✔Cover Letters For Dummies
  0-7645-5224-4
- ✔Frugal Living For Dummies
  0-7645-5403-4
- ✔Leadership For Dummies
  0-7645-5176-0
- ✔Managing For Dummies
  0-7645-1771-6

- ✔Marketing For Dummies
  0-7645-5600-2
- ✔Personal Finance For Dummies *
  0-7645-2590-5
- ✔Project Management For Dummies
  0-7645-5283-X
- ✔Resumes For Dummies †
  0-7645-5471-9
- ✔Selling For Dummies
  0-7645-5363-1
- ✔Small Business Kit For Dummies *†
  0-7645-5093-4

~~HO~~ME & BUSINESS COMPUTER BASICS

0-7645-4074-2

0-7645-3758-X

Also available:

- ✔ACT! 6 For Dummies
  0-7645-2645-6
- ✔iLife '04 All-in-One Desk Reference
  For Dummies
  0-7645-7347-0
- ✔iPAQ For Dummies
  0-7645-6769-1
- ✔Mac OS X Panther Timesaving
  Techniques For Dummies
  0-7645-5812-9
- ✔Macs For Dummies
  0-7645-5656-8

- ✔Microsoft Money 2004 For Dummies
  0-7645-4195-1
- ✔Office 2003 All-in-One Desk Reference
  For Dummies
  0-7645-3883-7
- ✔Outlook 2003 For Dummies
  0-7645-3759-8
- ✔PCs For Dummies
  0-7645-4074-2
- ✔TiVo For Dummies
  0-7645-6923-6
- ✔Upgrading and Fixing PCs For Dummies
  0-7645-1665-5
- ✔Windows XP Timesaving Techniques
  For Dummies
  0-7645-3748-2

F~~OD,~~ HOME, GARDEN, HOBBIES, MUSIC & PETS

0-7645-5295-3

0-7645-5232-5

Also available:

- ✔Bass Guitar For Dummies
  0-7645-2487-9
- ✔Diabetes Cookbook For Dummies
  0-7645-5230-9
- ✔Gardening For Dummies *
  0-7645-5130-2
- ✔Guitar For Dummies
  0-7645-5106-X
- ✔Holiday Decorating For Dummies
  0-7645-2570-0
- ✔Home Improvement All-in-One
  For Dummies
  0-7645-5680-0

- ✔Knitting For Dummies
  0-7645-5395-X
- ✔Piano For Dummies
  0-7645-5105-1
- ✔Puppies For Dummies
  0-7645-5255-4
- ✔Scrapbooking For Dummies
  0-7645-7208-3
- ✔Senior Dogs For Dummies
  0-7645-5818-8
- ✔Singing For Dummies
  0-7645-2475-5
- ✔30-Minute Meals For Dummies
  0-7645-2589-1

~~IN~~TERNET & DIGITAL MEDIA

0-7645-1664-7

0-7645-6924-4

Also available:

- ✔2005 Online Shopping Directory
  For Dummies
  0-7645-7495-7
- ✔CD & DVD Recording For Dummies
  0-7645-5956-7
- ✔eBay For Dummies
  0-7645-5654-1
- ✔Fighting Spam For Dummies
  0-7645-5965-6
- ✔Genealogy Online For Dummies
  0-7645-5964-8
- ✔Google For Dummies
  0-7645-4420-9

- ✔Home Recording For Musicians
  For Dummies
  0-7645-1634-5
- ✔The Internet For Dummies
  0-7645-4173-0
- ✔iPod & iTunes For Dummies
  0-7645-7772-7
- ✔Preventing Identity Theft For Dummies
  0-7645-7336-5
- ✔Pro Tools All-in-One Desk Reference
  For Dummies
  0-7645-5714-9
- ✔Roxio Easy Media Creator For Dummies
  0-7645-7131-1

~~Se~~parate Canadian edition also available
~~Se~~parate U.K. edition also available

~~Avail~~able wherever books are sold. For more information or to order direct: U.S. customers visit www.dummies.com or call 1-877-762-2974.
~~U.K.~~ customers visit www.wileyeurope.com or call 0800 243407. Canadian customers visit www.wiley.ca or call 1-800-567-4797.

SPORTS, FITNESS, PARENTING, RELIGION & SPIRITUALITY

0-7645-5146-9

0-7645-5418-2

Also available:

- Adoption For Dummies
  0-7645-5488-3
- Basketball For Dummies
  0-7645-5248-1
- The Bible For Dummies
  0-7645-5296-1
- Buddhism For Dummies
  0-7645-5359-3
- Catholicism For Dummies
  0-7645-5391-7
- Hockey For Dummies
  0-7645-5228-7

- Judaism For Dummies
  0-7645-5299-6
- Martial Arts For Dummies
  0-7645-5358-5
- Pilates For Dummies
  0-7645-5397-6
- Religion For Dummies
  0-7645-5264-3
- Teaching Kids to Read For Dummies
  0-7645-4043-2
- Weight Training For Dummies
  0-7645-5168-X
- Yoga For Dummies
  0-7645-5117-5

TRAVEL

0-7645-5438-7

0-7645-5453-0

Also available:

- Alaska For Dummies
  0-7645-1761-9
- Arizona For Dummies
  0-7645-6938-4
- Cancún and the Yucatán For Dummies
  0-7645-2437-2
- Cruise Vacations For Dummies
  0-7645-6941-4
- Europe For Dummies
  0-7645-5456-5
- Ireland For Dummies
  0-7645-5455-7

- Las Vegas For Dummies
  0-7645-5448-4
- London For Dummies
  0-7645-4277-X
- New York City For Dummies
  0-7645-6945-7
- Paris For Dummies
  0-7645-5494-8
- RV Vacations For Dummies
  0-7645-5443-3
- Walt Disney World & Orlando For Dummies
  0-7645-6943-0

GRAPHICS, DESIGN & WEB DEVELOPMENT

0-7645-4345-8

0-7645-5589-8

Also available:

- Adobe Acrobat 6 PDF For Dummies
  0-7645-3760-1
- Building a Web Site For Dummies
  0-7645-7144-3
- Dreamweaver MX 2004 For Dummies
  0-7645-4342-3
- FrontPage 2003 For Dummies
  0-7645-3882-9
- HTML 4 For Dummies
  0-7645-1995-6
- Illustrator CS For Dummies
  0-7645-4084-X

- Macromedia Flash MX 2004 For Dummies
  0-7645-4358-X
- Photoshop 7 All-in-One Desk
  Reference For Dummies
  0-7645-1667-1
- Photoshop CS Timesaving Techniques
  For Dummies
  0-7645-6782-9
- PHP 5 For Dummies
  0-7645-4166-8
- PowerPoint 2003 For Dummies
  0-7645-3908-6
- QuarkXPress 6 For Dummies
  0-7645-2593-X

NETWORKING, SECURITY, PROGRAMMING & DATABASES

0-7645-6852-3

0-7645-5784-X

Also available:

- A+ Certification For Dummies
  0-7645-4187-0
- Access 2003 All-in-One Desk
  Reference For Dummies
  0-7645-3988-4
- Beginning Programming For Dummies
  0-7645-4997-9
- C For Dummies
  0-7645-7068-4
- Firewalls For Dummies
  0-7645-4048-3
- Home Networking For Dummies
  0-7645-42796

- Network Security For Dummies
  0-7645-1679-5
- Networking For Dummies
  0-7645-1677-9
- TCP/IP For Dummies
  0-7645-1760-0
- VBA For Dummies
  0-7645-3989-2
- Wireless All In-One Desk Reference
  For Dummies
  0-7645-7496-5
- Wireless Home Networking For Dummies
  0-7645-3910-8